CORE FOCUS

GRADE 3

TEST PRACTICE
for Common Core

Susan M. Signet, M.A.

and

Renee Snyder, M.A.

BARRON'S

About the Authors

Susan M. Signet is an Intervention Specialist in Columbus, Ohio currently completing her sixth year of teaching Language Arts and Math to students in grades K–5 in a variety of settings. She has earned a Master's Degree in Teaching and Learning through The Ohio State University and completed her undergraduate degree from Wittenberg University.

Renee Snyder is a Professional Development Coordinator for the Teaching & Learning Collaborative in Columbus, Ohio. As a Professional Development Coordinator, Renee develops, coordinates, and facilitates professional learning opportunities for teachers across Ohio and other states focusing on Math, Science, and Technology. Renee earned a Master's Degree in Teaching and Learning from The Ohio State University and received her undergraduate degree in Early Childhood Education from Ohio University.

Acknowledgments

We want to extend our gratitude and appreciation to our many colleagues and mentors who have supported us in our professional endeavours and continuous learning. The collaboration with colleagues, administrators, and mentors across many districts, in addition to professional development opportunities, provided us with the content knowledge and numerous experiences to make this book possible. Thoughtful discussions, classroom reflections, and student analysis when implementing the Common Core State Standards refined our thinking about student learning and mastery. We are forever indebted to you, as you have shaped, guided, and fostered our teaching and learning of the Common Core State Standards. We are very thankful to the school districts in which we work and have worked, as they fostered our love for professional learning. To our family and friends, thank you for being supportive and inspiring us to reach our goals and take risks! We are extremely grateful to Peter Mavrikis, our Barron's Editor, for his guidance and personal attention throughout the development of this book.

All inquiries should be addressed to:
Barron's Educational Series, Inc.
250 Wireless Boulevard
Hauppauge, New York 11788
www.barronseduc.com

ISBN: 978-1-4380-0551-5
Library of Congress Control Number 2014946850

PRINTED IN THE UNITED STATES OF AMERICA
9 8 7 6 5 4 3 2

CONTENTS

ENGLISH LANGUAGE ARTS

Reading: Literature

Reading: Informational Text

Reading: Foundation Skills

Writing

Language

MATH

Operations and Algebraic Thinking

Number and Operations in Base Ten

Number and Operations—Fractions

Measurement and Data

Geometry

NOTE TO PARENTS AND EDUCATORS

About Barron's Core Focus Workbooks

Barron's recognizes the urgent need to create a product to help students navigate the Common Core State Standards being implemented in schools across America. To meet this need, we have created these grade-specific workbooks that will help bring the Common Core standards to life and ensure that students are prepared for these recently implemented assessments and expectations in learning. It is our hope that students can work through these books either independently or with the guidance of a parent or teacher.

Barron's Core Focus workbooks are meant to supplement the Common Core teaching that students are receiving in their classrooms or other learning environment. The books, all created by dedicated educators, provide specific practice on the Common Core standards through a variety of exercises and question types, including multiple-choice, short-answer, and extended-response. The questions are organized to build on each other, increasing student understanding from one standard to the next, one step at a time, and they challenge students to apply the standards in different formats. Both the English Language Arts (ELA) and Math sections of the books end with a review test—a great way to sum up what the student has learned and reviewed from the exercises throughout.

What Is Common Core?

"The standards are designed to be robust and relevant to the real world, reflecting the knowledge and skills that our young people need for success in college and careers."

(2012 Common Core State Standards Initiative)

Simply put, the Common Core is a series of standards that spell out exactly what students are expected to learn in English Language Arts and Mathematics throughout their years in school. These standards are fairly consistent across all grades and are designed so that students, teachers, and parents can understand what students should be learning and achieving at each grade level. Standards are organized to provide a clear understanding of the core concepts and procedures that students should master at each step of the way through school.

Unlike previous standards that were created by individual states, the Common Core is meant to be consistent throughout the country, providing students with an equal and fair opportunity to learn English Language Arts and Math. They have also been designed to teach students how to apply this knowledge to their everyday lives and experiences.

By sharing the same standards, states can more accurately gauge and compare students' progress and the quality of education received. The ultimate goal of Common Core is to ensure that all students, no matter which state or part of the country they are from, will be equally ready and prepared for college and the workforce.

What Is a Standard?

A standard is a skill that should be learned by a student. Standards are organized by *domains*, which are larger groupings of related standards. For instance, in grade 3 Math, there are five domains: "Operations and Algebraic Thinking," "Number and Operations in Base Ten," "Number and Operations—Fractions," "Measurement and Data," and "Geometry."

Under the domain "Operations and Algebraic Thinking," there are nine individual standards which highlight a specific skill or understanding that a student should gain. One standard, **OA.A.1**, directs students to "interpret products of whole numbers"—for example, learn and know that 5×7 represents the number of objects in 5 groups of 7 objects each.

Note that this book does not include practice for all of the Common Core standards but only for those standards that can be utilized in the workbook format. For example, "Speaking and Listening" is not covered in this workbook. This umbrella standard, which includes "ask and answer questions about information from a speaker" (SL.3.3) and "create engaging audio recordings of stories or poems" (SL.3.5), is more interactive, would work better in a group or classroom, and does not require the benefit of a workbook.

ENGLISH LANGUAGE ARTS

English Language Arts standards are separated into different strands. The K–5 standards are comprehensive and are divided into the following areas: Reading, Writing, Speaking and Listening, Foundational Skills, and Language. The Common Core has designated separate reading standards for both fiction and nonfiction texts. These standards are identified as Reading: Literature and Reading: Informational Text. Most importantly, the reading standards attempt to engage all students in the reading process. To meet the standards, students are expected to read multiple forms of text types, and in turn provide deeper literary experiences for all students. The Common Core also emphasizes the importance of text complexity. "Through extensive reading of stories, dramas, poems, and myths from diverse cultures and different time periods, students gain literary and cultural knowledge as well as familiarity with various text structures and elements." (2012 Common Core State Standards Initiative)

Each of the K–5 strands are arranged within a College and Career Readiness Anchor Standard. The Anchor Standards are the overarching goals of a K–12 curriculum. These standards remain constant in all grades. Each grade level's strands are built as a scaffold in order to achieve "official" College and Career Readiness Anchor Standards by the end of the twelfth grade. The College and Career Readiness Anchor Standards for reading literature and informational text focus on identifying key ideas and details, craft and structure, and the integration of knowledge and ideas. To meet the Common Core reading standards, students are expected to read, respond to, and interact with an array of text types of varying complexities. The College and Career Readiness Anchor Standards for writing focus on text types and purposes, production and distribution of writing, and research to build and present knowledge. To meet the Common Core writing standards, students are expected to write persuasive, narrative, and informational text. The College and Career Readiness Anchor Standards for speaking and listening focus on comprehension, collaboration, and presentation of knowledge and ideas. The speaking and listening standards focus heavily on students' ability to actively participate, engage, and present academic information in multiple settings. The College and Career Readiness Anchor Standards for language focus on the conventions of standard English, vocabulary acquisition, and knowledge of language.

The Common Core standards are also designed to help students create digital literature and use technology to communicate ideas and knowledge. The English Language Arts standards are a vision of what it means to be literate in the twenty-first century. These standards foster imperative learning experiences for the twenty-first century learner. "The skills and knowledge captured in the English Language Arts/literacy standards are designed to prepare students for life outside the classroom. They include critical-thinking skills and the ability to closely and attentively read texts in a way that will help them understand and enjoy complex works of literature." (2012 Common Core Initiative)

MATH

The Common Core mathematics standards were developed as a connected progression of learning throughout grades K–12. Ideally, this will enable teachers to close achievement gaps and give students the foundational skills necessary to continue in their learning. The Common Core provides teachers with an opportunity to build a deep and rich understanding of mathematical concepts. Instruction of Common Core mathematics standards encompasses the Mathematical Practices as well. These practices include skills that math students in every grade are expected to master. The Mathematical Practices bring rigor and rich learning opportunities to the classroom.

In grade 3, Number and Operations—Fractions is a new domain introduced to students. In grades 1 and 2, students learn fractional parts of a whole, which is located in the geometry domain for these grades. Then in grade 3, there is a shift in understanding, and students are expected to understand fractions as numbers, such as ¼, and understand that this means 1 part out of 4 equal parts. The Common Core standards are related across grade levels as well as across the domains. For example, Measurement and Data standards share a number of common relationships with the Operations and Algebra standards. This connectedness helps students prepare for the real world—remember, we don't use just one skill to balance our checkbook or determine the amount of paint for a room in our home. We have to be able to apply a variety of skills every day, and the goal of the Common Core math standards is to help prepare students for this. The Common Core also supports mathematical understanding of concepts that are developmentally appropriate for students. These standards allow students to build strong number sense in the early grades as they learn to count, order numbers, and compare numbers to help them think about numbers flexibly and understand the relationships between numbers as they move into the higher grades.

HOW TO USE THIS BOOK

This test practice workbook is organized by standard—one step at a time—in the order that students will likely see the concepts in the classroom or other learning environment. Each standard is organized in an easy-to-navigate spread(s) providing exposure to the Common Core in the simplest way possible.

In this book, students will be able to build skills in multiple formats by answering multiple-choice, short-answer, and extended-response questions. Answers and explanations are included at the end of each section so students, parents, and teachers can easily assess the student's response. These explanations are an important part of the learning process as they provide information on the understanding needed to answer each question, common misconceptions students have, and an explanation of how a student might best approach the question. Students using **Barron's Core Focus** workbooks will practice each of the specific content standards as they learn them, and also have the opportunity to review *all* of the concepts in Math or English Language Arts through the cumulative assessments.

In addition to the practice spreads covering specific standards, each section ends with a comprehensive practice test allowing students to monitor their general progress in either English Language Arts or Math. Answers and explanations provide additional guidance and instruction.

A complete listing of all the grade 3 English Language Arts and Math standards can be found at the end of this book in Appendices A and B.

FEATURES AND BENEFITS

Barron's Core Focus workbooks provide educators, parents, and students with an opportunity to enhance their knowledge and practice grade-level expectations with the Common Core English Language Arts and Math standards. Each workbook in this series provides questions that specifically correlate to each standard. Every answer explanation provides helpful insight into a student's understanding. The books also provide a cumulative assessment for each content area in Math and English Language Arts. Throughout the books, there are tip boxes that contain a variety of information and expose students to vocabulary, advice, and strategies.

- Parents can use this book to encourage learning at home. This book can be used as guided practice or extra exposure to concepts students may be struggling to master in school.

- Educators can use this book in their classrooms to identify how to assess each standard. Teachers will find that this book gives them insight into what students should be able to do independently in order to master the standard. The detailed answer explanations in the book provide opportunities for teachers to recognize misconceptions students may have regarding specific standards and how to successfully approach questions applicable to each standard.

- Students can use this book at home to build their knowledge of Math and English Language Arts content. They can practice the content they have learned, are learning, or are going to learn. This book can be used to prepare students for what's to come and/or as remedial information for concepts that are posing a particular challenge. The explanations in the book are extremely valuable to students as they work independently, increasing their awareness of concepts and improving their confidence as they work through each question.

The benefits that **Barron's Core Focus** workbooks will provide students, parents, and teachers are endless as the Common Core is implemented in schools across America.

Common Core State Standards Initiative
http://www.corestandards.org/

PARCC
http://www.parcconline.org/

Smarter Balance Assessment Consortium
www.smarterbalanced.org

ENGLISH LANGUAGE ARTS

The English Language Arts standards are separated into different strands. The K–5 standards are comprehensive and are divided into the following areas: Reading, Writing, Speaking and Listening, Foundational Skills, and Language. The Common Core has designated separate reading standards for both fiction and nonfiction texts. These standards are identified as Reading: Literature and Reading: Informational Text. In this section students will practice skills covering a variety of standards. Each section covers a specific standard covered in grade 3 and provides the student with practice through multiple-choice, short-answer, matching, and extended-response questions.

UNDERSTANDING TEXT

RL.3.1 Ask and answer questions to demonstrate understanding of a text, referring explicitly to the text as the basis for the answers.

Directions: Read the passages and answer the questions that follow.

Excerpt from *Crisis in Crittertown* by Justine Fontes.

The morning of The Change was no different. As soon as we realized we could understand humans, Grayson squeaked, "We must explore! Let's go upstairs and find out what they do at the post office."

Up until then we didn't know zip about zip codes. All we knew about the postal service was when the workers came and went, and what they left in the trash cans.

"No one's going anywhere!" our leader squeaked firmly. Brownback was a cautious mouse. Like his son, he was mostly gray, but with a stripe of brown down his back. His muzzle fur was white with age. We all respected him greatly—except Grayson.

> Don't forget to go back into the story to help you find your answers.

"Ah, Pops! There's so much to learn. It could benefit the colony. I'll be careful," Grayson promised. "I won't make a sound or let anyone see me. I'll…even take Cheddar along."

To my surprise, this last phrase changed Brownback's expression.

Grayson saw that, too, because he squeaked on. "He'll keep me in line. You know Cheddar. He's always holding me back from fun…I mean danger."

Brownback nodded. "Cheddar is cautious, and caution keeps a mouse alive."

I felt flattered. "Cautious" sounds so much better than "coward."

Grayson seized on this. "We won't stay long. We'll come home with lots of news for you."

Brownback always said, "Facts help a leader make good decisions." He liked news almost as much as I like cheese. Brownback nodded. "You and Cheddar may go upstairs."

Grayson jumped so high, even his tail left the ground.

Brownback sighed. "Calm down, boy." Then he told me, "Don't let him do anything foolish."

I nodded, suddenly realizing what had happened. What happened?! When had I agreed to go upstairs?

This was even scarier than the time Grayson talked me into helping him use a pencil to trip a trap. I shuddered at that memory. How did I let him get me into these things?

1. Using what you have read, what do you infer "The Change" is?

    Ⓐ A change in temperature

    Ⓑ A change in the mice's ability to understand humans

    Ⓒ A change in the mice's home

    Ⓓ A change in the mice's leadership

2. Why does Brownback let Grayson go when he says he will take Cheddar along?

    Ⓐ Cheddar has a good sense of direction so they will not get lost.

    Ⓑ Cheddar understands the human's language.

    Ⓒ Cheddar is cautious and will keep them out of trouble.

    Ⓓ Cheddar is his best friend.

3. How is Cheddar feeling about going to explore the post office? Use a detail from the text to support your thinking.

Cheddar's Feeling	
Supporting Detail	

4. Why are Cheddar and Grayson exploring the post office?

   _____

   _____

5. What do you think will happen next in the story?

(A) Cheddar and Grayson will leave to explore the post office.

(B) The mice will find a new place to live.

(C) Brownback will go out instead to explore the post office.

(D) A cat will chase after the mice in the colony.

Excerpt from *Panda Panic: Running Wild* by Jamie Rixx.

Ping had decided to give surfing another try. He was well aware that his last effort had ended rather soggily, with water being squeezed out of his tail and shaken out of his ears at the veterinarian's office, but that was a long time ago. He was two weeks older now and much, much wiser. Besides, he'd done a lot of thinking about what went wrong on that occasion and had decided that it was all the fault of his surfboard—not its rider. He needed a *single* piece of wood instead of a tray made from bamboo poles lashed together—a big, flexible board that could withstand the pressures that a champion surfer would demand from it. As luck would have it, five minutes later, as he wandered past the tall ranger's office, he stumbled upon the perfect piece of wood lying across his path. Someone had even customized it for him by painting it bright green. He went to knock on the back door of the office to ask if he might take it, but to his surprise there *was* no door, just a hole in the wall where a door had once been. He waited outside the office for a couple of minutes, but nobody came, so he helped himself and, clamping his new surfboard underneath his arm, he set off for the River Trickle.

6. What do you infer the "perfect piece of wood" actually is that Ping found?

    Ⓐ A surfboard

    Ⓑ The door from the ranger's office

    Ⓒ A sofa cushion

    Ⓓ A rug

7. Why does Ping think his surfing did not go well last time?

    Ⓐ The waves were not big enough.

    Ⓑ It rained on him.

    Ⓒ He didn't have a good surfboard.

    Ⓓ He hadn't surfed very much before.

8. What is the main idea of this section?

_____

_____

9. What detail from the text tells why Ping thinks a single piece of wood will make a better surfboard?

_____

_____

10. Write a question you are wondering about after reading this excerpt from *Panda Panic: Running Wild*.

_____

_____

(Answers on pages 71–72)

FABLES, FOLKTALES, AND MYTHS

RL.3.2 Recount stories, including fables, folktales, and myths from diverse cultures; determine the central message, lesson, or moral and explain how it is conveyed through key details in the text.

Directions: Read the passage and answer the questions below.

The Crow and the Pitcher by Aesop.

It was a sweltering, hot summer day. A crow, parched with thirst, came upon a pitcher of water. But the pitcher was only half full. The crow leaned and stretched and thrust out his beak as far as he could. No matter how hard he tried, he could not reach the water.

All of a sudden, the crow had an idea. He picked up a pebble in his beak and dropped it into the water. The water level in the pitcher rose just a tiny bit. So he dropped in another pebble, then another, then one more. The crow continued doing this for a long time. Finally, the water in the pitcher had risen high enough. The crow poked in his beak and drank to his heart's content!

> Make sure to think about what the characters are learning in the story to determine the moral or lesson.

1. Using the details from *The Crow and the Pitcher*, complete the sequence of events below:

   (1) The crow is thirsty so he tries to drink from the pitcher but the water is too low.

   (2) _____

   (3) The water starts to rise in the pitcher.

   (4) _____

2. What was the problem in this fable?

   Ⓐ The crow was really hot.

   Ⓑ The sun was shining on the crow.

   Ⓒ The water in the pitcher was too low.

   Ⓓ The crow was thirsty and there was no water.

3. What is the lesson in the fable *The Crow and the Pitcher*?

   _____

   _____

4. Which detail helps to convey the lesson in this passage?

   Ⓐ "The crow continued doing this for a long time."

   Ⓑ "All of a sudden, the crow had an idea."

   Ⓒ "No matter how hard he tried, he could not reach the water."

   Ⓓ "The crow poked in his beak."

5. What would be another good title for this fable?

   Ⓐ Pebble by Pebble

   Ⓑ A Really Hot Day

   Ⓒ How Animals Get Water

   Ⓓ Water

(Answers on page 72)

CHARACTERS

Directions: Read the passages and answer the questions that follow.

Excerpt from *Night at the Museum* by Leslie Goldman.

Larry Daley was having a bad day. Lately, he'd been having a string of bad days. They added up to not just a bad week or a bad month, but actually, a fairly bad few years. Yet, today was even worse than usual. Today, they'd shut off his cable.

Larry hadn't paid the bill, but was that any reason to deny him television? He didn't think so, which is why he called the cable company to try and reason with them.

"Hello, Delores, this is Larry Daley. You guys shut off my cable yesterday. I know the bill is late, but we've just had some minor organizational problems over here."

Larry was stretching the truth. His problems were major, not minor. He wasn't organized in the slightest. His apartment was a huge mess. It was filled with a jumble of books and papers, hockey equipment, and boxes. One look at his apartment and a person would think he'd either just moved in or was about to move out. In fact, neither was the case.

1. What do Larry's choices as a character tell you about him?
   - Ⓐ He is not responsible.
   - Ⓑ He has had bad days.
   - Ⓒ He cares about his cable bill.
   - Ⓓ You should feel bad because he has a lot of bad days.

2. Larry said, "...we've just had some minor organizational problems over here." How does this describe him as a character?

Ⓐ He misplaced his bills.

Ⓑ He is forgetful.

Ⓒ He is telling the truth.

Ⓓ He is making excuses about paying the bill.

3. How does the narrator of the story describe Larry's character?

Ⓐ He is a slob.

Ⓑ He just moved in to a new apartment.

Ⓒ He is packing to move to a new home.

Ⓓ He collects hockey equipment.

4. Would you want to be Larry's friend? Explain your reasoning.

_____

_____

Excerpt from *Night at the Museum* by Leslie Goldman.

"Let's see. Keys, flashlight... I feel like I'm forgetting something," said Cecil. "Ah yes! The instruction manual." Cecil pulled a thick stack of legal paper out of his bag. It was stapled together, dog-eared, and frayed. There were handwritten scribbles all over the cover and complicated-looking diagrams inside. Cecil handed it to Larry as if it were a precious, one-of-a-kind book.

"Larry, it is crucial you follow these instructions. Crucial," he said.

"Guys, come on," said Larry. He wondered if this were yet another joke. "I can walk around an empty museum holding a flashlight. It's gonna be okay."

"There's a little more to it than that, son," said Reginald.

Gus pointed to the manual. He was pretty serious. "Start at number one. Then number two. Then go to number three. Then—"

Larry interrupted. "Let me guess, number four."

"Are you cracking wise?" asked Gus. "Because I will sock you in your nose, tough guy."

"Leave him alone," said Reginald. "You got it covered, right, Larry?"

"I just follow the instructions," said Larry.

"Do them all. Do them in order. Do them quick. And the most important thing to remember is don't let anything in... or out," said Cecil.

Larry stared at him, wondering what he was talking about. This was a museum, after all. It wasn't a zoo!

5. How does Reginald help Larry understand that he needs to take Cecil's advice seriously?

Ⓐ Larry thinks they are playing a joke on him.

Ⓑ Larry thinks he knows everything about the museum.

Ⓒ Reginald tells Larry that there is more to being a guard than carrying a flashlight and keys.

Ⓓ Gus makes Larry believe that Cecil wants to play a trick on Larry.

6. How does Cecil's language in the passage show his feelings about Larry being a guard?

Ⓐ He is the boss of the museum.

Ⓑ He is caring and wants to make sure Larry is prepared for his new job.

Ⓒ He wants to quickly give Larry a tour, so he can go home.

Ⓓ He does not know how to help Larry learn the job.

7. What challenges do you think Larry will face in his new job at the museum?

Ⓐ Following instructions

Ⓑ Giving guests at the museum information

Ⓒ Taking care of the sculptures

Ⓓ Cleaning the museum after hours

Once he was by himself, Larry sat down at the information desk and put the instruction manual in front of him. He leaned toward it, as if to begin reading. Instead, he decided to rest his head on it. It wasn't the most comfortable of pillows, but he'd definitely slept on worse.

Soon Larry was snoring so loudly, he woke himself up. He opened his eyes just in time to see a shiny blue beetle skitter across the floor.

It was strange looking, but Larry didn't think twice. Standing up, he stretched. Then he headed for the men's room. He had to cross the main lobby, where the T-Rex skeleton should have been. Larry walked right past it, not even noticing that it had vanished. As soon as he got into the men's room, he realized something was wrong. Larry went back outside. He did a double take. Still, no T-Rex skeleton.

8. Did Larry listen to the other characters' advice from the previous passage? Justify your thinking.

_____

_____

9. What did Cecil tell Larry that contributed to the events in the second passage?
   (A) Cecil told him to sit at the front desk.
   (B) Cecil told him to walk around the museum.
   (C) Cecil told him to start at number 1 in the manual and then read number two, and then go to number 3.
   (D) Cecil told him to do all of the instructions, do them in order, and do them quick.

10. How would Cecil feel about Larry now in the story?
    (A) Disappointed that he did not read the manual
    (B) Proud that he walked the museum
    (C) Delighted that he sat down at the information desk
    (D) Thankful that he realized something was wrong

(Answers on pages 72–73)

THE MEANING OF WORDS AND PHRASES

RL.3.4. Determine the meaning of words and phrases as they are used in a text, distinguishing literal from nonliteral language.

Directions: Answer the questions below.

1. Determine the meaning of the bolded phrase in the following text.

   Seeing these machines in motion **filled me with awe**. How did people make such things?

   _____

   _____

2. Grayson squeaked, "I wish I were big enough to drive!"
   I sighed. "Yes, I'm sure you'd like to drive very fast."
   Grayson smiled. "You know me so well."
   We were bald, blind infants together. Of course I knew him.
   I even liked him more than anyone else—when he wasn't
   scaring the fur off me.

   Determine the meaning of the bolded phrase above.
   (A) Making him very scared
   (B) Making him start to shed his fur
   (C) Making him tear his fur out
   (D) Making him content and peaceful

3. So we stayed until the mail carriers left on their **routes**. The carriers were the people who drove the mail to all the homes and businesses in Crittertown.

   What part of the sentences above helps you know what **"routes"** are?

   _____

   _____

4. I couldn't smell cheese, but I sensed its presence. Maybe cheese sends out a frequency, like a TV broadcast. Maybe my stomach is tuned to the cheese channel.

What does the mouse compare his ability to sense cheese to?

_____

_____

5. I looked around the parking lot. Staying there alone was almost as scary as following Grayson. Besides, I'd promised Brownback to keep both eyes on his grandson. I scurried under the door after my friend.

> Literal—when the words used represent and have their exact meaning.
>
> Nonliteral—when the words used have a different meaning than their exact wording (also known as *figurative language*).

We **caught our breath** in the back room with the coats. We sniffed and listened. I smelled the postmaster's coffee and the clerk's perfume.

What detail helps the reader know what the phrase **caught our breath** means?

Ⓐ I looked around the parking lot.

Ⓑ I scurried under the door after my friend.

Ⓒ We sniffed and listened.

Ⓓ I'd promised Brownback to keep both eyes on his grandson.

6. "Let's find out!" Grayson replied. Then he slid under the torn rubber trim at the bottom of the post office's **rickety** back door.

What detail in the sentences above helps the reader know what the word **rickety** means?

_____

_____

(Answers on page 73)

STORY VOCABULARY
AND ORDER

> **RL.3.5** Refer to parts of stories, dramas, and poems when writing or speaking about a text, using terms such as chapter, scene, and stanza; describe how each successive part builds on earlier sections.

Directions: Read and answer the questions below.

1. A stanza is to poetry like a paragraph is to _____
   - Ⓐ a story
   - Ⓑ words
   - Ⓒ a text feature
   - Ⓓ a topic

2. Why does an author organize a story into chapters for the reader?
   - Ⓐ To help the reader understand the characters.
   - Ⓑ To support what is being read by putting the text in a logical order.
   - Ⓒ To allow the reader to understand scene changes.
   - Ⓓ To encourage the reader to infer character traits.

3. Why does a poet use line breaks in a poem?
   - Ⓐ To allow the reader to take extra breaths.
   - Ⓑ To help the reader read fluently.
   - Ⓒ To help the reader use expression.
   - Ⓓ To enhance the meaning of ideas, thoughts, or words in a poem.

> Texts have a structure that provides organization to help the reader make sense about ideas, thoughts, and events. Different genres of writing organize these elements in various ways.

4. True or False: When writing a fiction story an author usually organizes the story by telling the solution to the problem, then the characters, then the problem and finally they describe the setting.

   True   **False**

5. Why would you need to read about the characters in the story before reading the solution to the problem?

   _____

   _____

The Boy Who Never Told a Lie
Once there was a little boy,
　With curly hair and pleasant eye—
A boy who always told the truth,
　And never, never told a lie.

And when he trotted off to school,
　The children all about would cry,
"There goes the curly-headed boy—
　The boy that never tells a lie."

And everybody loved him so,
　Because he always told the truth,
That every day, as he grew up,
　'Twas said, "There goes the honest youth."

And when the people that stood near
　Would turn to ask the reason why,
The answer would be always this:
　"Because he never tells a lie."

6. How many stanzas are in this poem?
Ⓐ 16　　　　　　　Ⓒ 7
Ⓑ 2　　　　　　　Ⓓ 4

7. Explain how you can use the first and second stanza to understand what is happening to the boy and his characteristics in the third stanza.

_____

_____

(Answers on pages 73–74)

POINT OF VIEW

RL.3.6 Distinguish their own point of view from that of the narrator or those of the characters.

Directions: Read and answer the questions below.

1. What does it mean when a story is written in first person?
   - (A) The story is about the first character mentioned.
   - (B) The story is written using words such as I, me, and we.
   - (C) The story is written using words such as he, she, him, and her.
   - (D) The story's only character is the narrator.

2. What is a story's point of view?
   - (A) The perspective from which the story is being told.
   - (B) How the character feels.
   - (C) The purpose of the story.
   - (D) The lesson or moral the story is teaching.

Directions: Read the passage below and answer the questions.

My Name is Bob by Gerald Kelley.

I ran and ran through the crowded streets, not knowing where I was. That night I slid inside a cardboard box in the doorway of a shop. It was warm and cozy and it made me think of home. "I miss curling up in my chair. How I miss my home," I thought.

The next morning a big man woke me up. "Scram!" he shouted, shaking me out of my box. I ran away.

Days passed. Everywhere I went, people chased me off.

Weeks passed. I crept away and hid.

And then one morning I heard a friendly voice. "Hello, pussycat, do you want to come home with me?" "Yes please," I purred. I was so happy that someone wanted me.

But his mother wouldn't let me in. "I'm not having that smelly cat in my house," she said, and she slammed the door closed.

3. From what point of view is the passage written?
   (A) Second person
   (C) First person
   (B) Third person
   (D) Fourth person

4. Who is the narrator of the passage?
   (A) A mother
   (C) A young boy
   (B) A cat
   (D) A big man

5. What is the problem in the passage that influences the reader's point of view?
   (A) The character doesn't have a home.
   (B) The character is not liked by the street cats.
   (C) The character is lost.
   (D) The character cannot sleep.

6. How does the narrator feel in the story?
   (A) Lonely
   (C) Warm
   (B) Content
   (D) Curious

7. How does the author make you as a reader feel about the cat? Use evidence from the text.

   _____

   _____

8. What does the mother not know about the cat that may change her point of view?
   (A) He lived in a box.
   (C) He likes music.
   (B) He used to live in a home.
   (D) He is scared of others.

9. In the passage, from whom do you gain insight on the point of view?
   (A) The narrator
   (C) The pizza man
   (B) The boy
   (D) A box

(Answers on pages 74–75)

TEXT ILLUSTRATIONS

RL.3.7 Explain how specific aspects of a text's illustrations contribute to what is conveyed by the words in a story (e.g., create mood, emphasize aspects of a character or setting).

1. The illustrations of a text

   Ⓐ convey meaning   Ⓒ both a. and b.

   Ⓑ sets the mood   Ⓓ none of the above

2. Based on the illustration below, what can you infer about the characters?

   Ⓐ They are worried about grandpa.

   Ⓑ They are playing a game.

   Ⓒ They are eager to find grandpa.

   Ⓓ They are catching animals.

   > The illustrations in a text help the reader gain new ideas and make connections between characters, settings, chapters, and texts.

The twins were looking for their grandfather.

He wasn't in the woodshed.

3. What does it mean when an illustrator uses vibrant colors?

   Ⓐ A scary event is happening.   Ⓒ The plot is mysterious.

   Ⓑ A character is sad.   Ⓓ Characters are excited.

4. How does the illustration help you relate to how Papa
Chagall's father feels about his paintings?

Ⓐ His father is intrigued by his paintings.

Ⓑ His father thinks he is creative.

Ⓒ His father likes his imagination.

Ⓓ His father thinks his paintings are meaningless.

5. What meaning do the rounded shapes in the illustration convey
to you?

Ⓐ The shapes create comfort.

Ⓑ The shapes show tension.

Ⓒ The shapes create a gloomy picture.

Ⓓ The shapes are creative.

6. What is the mood the artist is trying to convey in the illustration below?

   Ⓐ The man is lost.

   Ⓑ The man is using his imagination.

   Ⓒ The man met the love of his life.

   Ⓓ The woman is a fairy.

One day I was coming home and I saw a girl standing on a bridge. Her name was Bella, which means beautiful.

As soon as I saw her, I knew that Bella was the one for me.

7. How does the illustration emphasize Papa Chagall's feelings toward Bella as stated in the text?

_____

_____

8. How do the colors in an illustration help to create the mood of the text?

_____

9. In the illustration, Papa Chagall and his wife are flying. What is implied about how the characters are feeling in this part of the story?

Ⓐ Papa Chagall and his wife are happy because they are now married.

Ⓑ Papa Chagall and his wife are scared.

Ⓒ Papa Chagall and his wife are trying to leave.

Ⓓ Papa Chagall just got a new painting job.

"And that's how I met your granny. Look, come inside, I'll show you the painting I made. It's called *The Birthday*."

"Why are you flying?" said the twins.

"We are flying because we are so happy," said Papa Chagall.

Illustrations from *Papa Chagall, Tell Us a Story* by Laurence Anholt and published by Frances Lincoln Ltd, copyright © 2014. Reproduced by permission of Frances Lincoln Ltd.

(Answers on pages 75–76)

UNDERSTANDING TEXT

RI.3.1 Ask and answer questions to demonstrate understanding of a text, referring explicitly to the text as the basis for the answers.

Directions: Read the passage and answer the questions below.

The Northern Sea Lion

Northern sea lions, also known as Stellar sea lions, live in the Northern Pacific Ocean. Their range stretches from Japan to California. Adult males weigh between 1,300 and 2,500 pounds and can grow to about 9 to 10 feet in length. Most females weigh about 1,000 pounds and can grow to be 7 to 8 feet long.

Before the Marine Mammal Protection Act was put into law in 1972, these sea lions were hunted for food. They were also killed for their fur, which was used for clothing. Since 1972, this law has made it illegal to hunt the Northern sea lion in the United States. It has also made it illegal for other countries to take marine mammals, such as the sea lion, from U.S. waters. Despite these protections, the Northern sea lion remains endangered. In addition to the hunting that still occurs, their habitats have been affected by pollution and their food source, other fish, has been reduced due to overfishing.

1. Stellar sea lions live in the
   - Ⓐ Mediterranean Sea
   - Ⓑ South Atlantic
   - Ⓒ Northern Pacific Ocean
   - Ⓓ Gulf of Mexico

2. True or False. Adult female Northern sea lions weigh more than the adult males.

   True   **False**

3. The Northern sea lion is also known as the
   - Ⓐ Guadalupe fur seal
   - Ⓑ New Zealand sea lion
   - Ⓒ Stellar sea lion
   - Ⓓ Phocid

4. List two problems that are causing the Northern sea lion to become an endangered species.

1. _____

2. _____

Directions: Use the text below to answer questions 5–7.

Protecting the Seal

People have been hunting seals for at least 5,000 years. Seals are valuable to hunters because of their pelts, blubber, meat, and bones. Today, seal hunting is legal in only five countries: Canada, Greenland, Norway, Russia, and Namibia. None of the countries that allow seal hunting permit the hunting of endangered species of seals. Each year, these countries set quotas, which is the overall number of seals that can be killed. Quotas are used to make sure that people do not excessively overhunt seals and cause the populations to become endangered.

Some people would like all seal hunting to be illegal. Conservationists are hard at work on this and other key issues to protect seals and their habitats.

5. All of these countries still hunt seals EXCEPT
  Ⓐ Canada   Ⓒ Russia
  Ⓑ United States of America   Ⓓ Namibia

6. List two reasons why seals are hunted.

1. _____

2. _____

7. Why do the countries set quotas for the number of seals that can be hunted?

_____

_____

(Answers on page 76)

MAIN IDEA AND DETAILS

RI.3.2 Determine the main idea of a text; recount the key details and explain how they support the main idea.

Directions: Read the passage and answer the questions below.

A Touch of the Wild

Pet cats can bring a touch of wild nature into our lives and homes. This is because the domestic cat has changed very little from its wild ancestor. A house cat sleeping on the couch can instantly turn into a deadly hunter if it senses a mouse or any other small animal nearby. In fact, the house cat has been called one of nature's most perfect hunters.

To help them hunt, cats have very strong senses of hearing and vision. They hear much better than humans or dogs. Cats move their ears around to catch the tiniest sounds. They also have excellent vision. Cats can see the slightest movements from the corners of their eyes, so it can be hard for even an insect to go by undetected.

Cats often hunt at night. In low light, they are able to see ten times better than people do. Cats also have a better sense of smell than people. They use this sense mainly to get information about other cats that may be nearby. Whiskers also provide cats with important information. They use their whiskers much like radar to help them move around at night without bumping into things. In fact, whiskers are so sensitive that cats can even detect changes in the air!

1. Which of the following best describes the main idea of the passage?
   Ⓐ Cats have a strong sense of hearing.
   Ⓑ People can see ten times better than cats.
   Ⓒ Cats have changed very little from the time of their wild ancestors.
   Ⓓ Cats are very good hunters.

2. How did you find the main idea of the passage?

_____

_____

_____

3. List two details that support the main idea.

1. _____

2. _____

4. How are the supporting details related to the main idea?

_____

_____

5. What is another title that could be used to rename this passage?
- Ⓐ The Perfect Hunter
- Ⓑ Cats in the Wild
- Ⓒ Kitty Radar
- Ⓓ Hunting in Packs

6. What modern technology is similar to a cat's whiskers?
- Ⓐ Computer
- Ⓑ Automobile
- Ⓒ Radar
- Ⓓ Cell phone

7. List two senses that cats rely on when hunting.

1. _____

2. _____

(Answers on page 77)

RELATIONSHIPS BETWEEN TEXTS

RI.3.3 Describe the relationship between a series of historical events, scientific ideas or concepts, or steps in technical procedures in a text, using language that pertains to time, sequence, and cause/effect.

Directions: Read the passages and answer the questions below.

The Human Brain

The brain is the body's most complex organ. It is because of your brain that you are able to learn, think, speak, plan, and control everything from how you move your body to what you feel.

When you describe how passages are related, think about what makes them the same and different.

On the Job

Your brain is always working. It allows you to think, learn, remember, communicate, and react. It helps process the information you receive from the world around you and instructs other parts of the body on what they should do in response. The brain is doing its job even when you are sleeping. It controls body functions that we take for granted, including your heart rate, breathing, and even your dreams.

It's All in Your Head

Your brain is your body's computer. Since it plays such an important role, the body does its best to protect this important organ. Your brain is kept safe by the hard bones that form your skull. Beneath your skull, this soft, spongy organ floats in a liquid that helps protect it from infection, and also acts as a shock absorber against sudden physical impact.

Right Down the Middle

The brain is divided right down the middle into two equal parts. The two parts are called the left hemisphere (for the left part) and the right hemisphere (for the right part). Both these parts are connected by millions of neural fibers that help both parts of the brain to communicate. In a strange twist, the left hemisphere controls the right side of your body and the right hemisphere controls the left.

1. How are the passages "On the Job" and "Right Down the Middle" similar?

   _____

   _____

2. How are the passages "On the Job" and "Right Down the Middle" different?

   _____

   _____

3. How are all of these passages related?

   _____

   _____

4–5. Describe the main idea of each section from the passage to demonstrate the different scientific information in each section.

   4. "It's All in Your Head"

   _____

   5. "Right Down the Middle"

   _____

6. Why did the author include a few sentences of opening text before the section "On the Job"? How does it help you understand the sections that follow?

   _____

   _____

   _____

7. Describe a cause and effect relationship from the section, "On the Job."

   Cause: _____

   Effect: _____

(Answers on pages 77–78)

TEXT FEATURES AND SEARCH TOOLS

RI.3.5 Use text features and search tools (e.g., key words, sidebars, hyperlinks) to locate information relevant to a given topic efficiently.

1. In a nonfiction text, a table of contents can provide you with
   - (A) The name of the author of the book.
   - (B) What a book will be about.
   - (C) What information is in a book and where it is located.
   - (D) Where the reader can find more information about the same topic.

   > Nonfiction texts have features that help you find information quickly. These features vary with different texts.

2. An index is a nonfiction text feature that
   - (A) Lists topics in the book
   - (B) Provides a list of key words and topics in the book and the pages where they can be found
   - (C) Has words and definitions
   - (D) Has other resources the reader can use to understand a topic better

3. How can a search box help you find information efficiently when reading text on a website?
   - (A) A reader can use a search box to look for specific topics, words, and ideas quickly.
   - (B) A reader can use a search box to make connections to other websites.
   - (C) A reader can use a search box to ask questions.
   - (D) A search box is not a helpful tool for a reader.

4. Which of the following statements is not true about a hyperlink?
   - (A) A hyperlink is used to help the reader connect to new information.
   - (B) A hyperlink can be used in a book.
   - (C) A hyperlink can be used in a digital text.
   - (D) Not every digital text has a hyperlink.

5. Circle True or False: An icon is a word or image on a digital document or text that can help connect you to new information.

True   **False**

6. Explain how features of a nonfiction text can help you as the reader locate information quickly.

_____

_____

7. How are headings and subheadings related text features?
   Ⓐ A heading is the main idea of a text.
   Ⓑ A subheading is the keywords that are in the text.
   Ⓒ A subheading has detailed information about graphs, maps, charts, and diagrams.
   Ⓓ A subheading gives the reader information about key topics in a particular section of the text that can be found under a heading.

Directions: Read the passage and answer the question below.

Finding Fossils

Some fossils are found in the cold regions of the planet or in places where the ground is permanently frozen. Many of these discoveries contain plants and animals that lived during the **ice age**. These fossils come from organisms that died, froze, and remained undisturbed until the time they were discovered and **extracted**. Some of these finds include mammoths, saber-toothed cats, and ancient ferns.

8. In the passage, the author made the words **ice age** and **extracted** bold. What feature in the text could you use to find more information about the meaning of these words?
   Ⓐ Glossary   Ⓒ Dictionary
   Ⓑ Index   Ⓓ Thesaurus

(Answers on page 78)

POINT OF VIEW

Directions: Read the passage and answer the questions below.

Wetlands

Millions of plants and animals live in the wetlands around the world. Wetlands are also an important resource, providing food, building materials, and other products that people need and use every day. However, this important ecosystem is in trouble. More than half of the world's wetlands have been lost. People have drained the water to make room for houses, roads, and farms. Wetlands have also been damaged by pesticides used on farms, chemicals used in factories, and oil spills at sea.

Today we know that a healthy world depends on healthy wetlands. Scientists are learning more about wetlands and the plants and animals that live there. Conservation groups are working hard to protect the wetlands and to educate the public about the effects of their loss. Many governments around the world are also taking steps to save and restore wetlands. Unfortunately, for some places, it may already be too late to reverse the damage caused by years of neglect and misuse.

1. A point of view of a text is
   Ⓐ The author's way of thinking or position on a subject.
   Ⓑ The author using opinions to persuade the reader.
   Ⓒ The author sharing facts about real-life experiences.
   Ⓓ What the author teaches the reader of a nonfiction text.

2. What does the word *important* tell you about the author's point of view in the text?
   Ⓐ The author is using facts.
   Ⓑ The author is using opinions.
   Ⓒ The author is using facts and opinions.
   Ⓓ The author is using his or her personal experience.

3. In the passage, what is the author's point of view about wetlands?
   (A) Saving the wetlands can be costly.
   (B) In order to have a healthy planet we need to protect the world's wetlands.
   (C) Conservation efforts are too late to have any effect on wetlands.
   (D) Wetlands are home to many deadly plants and animals and should be destroyed.

4. In the text, what words are used to show the author's point of view about caring for wetlands?
   (A) Unfortunately, for some places, it may
   (B) Millions of plants and animals live in
   (C) Wetlands are also an important resource
   (D) Scientists are learning more about

5. Think about the information the author provided you as a reader in the text. Do you agree or disagree with the author's thinking? Explain.

   _____

   _____

   _____

6. What information did the author include in the text that influenced your point of view?

   _____

   _____

7. Does the reader's point of view need to be the same as the author's? Explain your reasoning.

   _____

   _____

(Answers on pages 78–79)

MAKING CONNECTIONS

RI.3.8 Describe the logical connection between particular sentences and paragraphs in a text (e.g., comparison, cause/effect, first/second/third in a sequence).

Directions: Answer the questions below.

1. Which graphic organizer would help you with a comparison text?

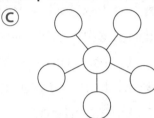

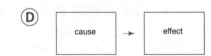

Directions: Use the following word bank for questions 2–7. Fill in the blanks to describe each text structure.

Word Bank: Compare/Contrast; Cause/Effect; Description; Problem/Solution; Sequence; Question/Answer.

2. The _____ text structure presents similarities and differences between two or more topics.

3. The _____ text structure presents a question and then provides an answer to the question.

4. The _____ text structure presents events in chronological or numerical order.

5. The _____ text structure presents ideas, facts, or events as a cause and then the result of this cause.

6. The _____ text structure provides information about a topic.

32

7. The _____ text structure presents a problem and then lists one or more solutions to the problem.

8. Match the following text structures to its example below.

_____ Cause and Effect   _____ Description

_____ Sequence   _____ Question and Answer

_____ Compare and Contrast   _____ Problem and Solution

A. When you are cooking pancakes, first you should mix up the batter, then you need to pour ¼ cup of batter onto a griddle to cook, finally when the bubbles start to pop flip your pancake and cook until it is light brown.

B. You might wonder what makes a plant grow the best. You need to make sure that your plant has plenty of sunlight, water, and good soil to grow in.

C. Dogs and cats both make great pets. Cats can spend most of their day inside and only need a litter box, food, and toys to play with. Dogs need to go outside for walks and to go to the bathroom.

D. When it snows a lot outside the roads can become slippery and dangerous. People drive slower and more carefully as a result of the snow.

E. Watermelons are a delicious fruit that grows on a vine. They have a green outside and red juicy fruit inside. They can have seeds or can be seedless. They are sweet-tasting.

F. Dogs love to dig holes, but this can be a problem if they dig up your yard. You can keep them from digging holes by training them to know that you do not like this behavior.

9. What word signals that a sequential text structure is being used?
   Ⓐ Because   Ⓑ Including   Ⓒ However   Ⓓ Finally

10. What word signals that a compare-and-contrast text structure is being used?
   Ⓐ Solution   Ⓑ Similarity   Ⓒ After   Ⓓ Second

(Answers on pages 79–80)

COMPARE AND CONTRAST

RI.3.9 Compare and contrast the most important points and key details presented in two texts on the same topic.

Directions: Read the passages and answer the questions that follow.

It's Not Easy Being Green

A frog's life begins when a female frog lays her eggs near a source of water, such as a pond or lake. Depending on the frog, she may have anywhere from just a few to thousands of eggs. This is the first stage of a frog's life. Some of the eggs will hatch after only a few days. Others will take weeks. Many of the eggs will be eaten by other animals. This is only the beginning of the struggles a frog will face before eventually reaching adulthood.

> Compare = Same
>
> Contrast = Different

When a frog egg hatches, what comes out is more like a fish than a frog. This is the larva stage. A frog larva is called a tadpole. Much like a fish, a tadpole has gills, fins, and a tail. It is during this period where young frogs face their greatest threat. Because they have not yet developed their legs and are very slow, tadpoles are easy to catch . . . and eat. Some animals that eat tadpoles can be as large as a raccoon. Others can be as small as a dragonfly larva. As the tadpole matures, only a small number will survive into adulthood. At this final stage of development, a tadpole turns into a frog. An adult frog changes completely, replacing its gills with lungs, dropping its fins and tail, and growing front and hind legs. Now, with these changes, a frog has a better chance of surviving against a threat. With strong hind legs, a frog can at least jump out of harm's way.

The Life of a Dragonfly

People often see dragonflies when they are walking near a pond, fishing in a stream, or swimming in a lake. That's because dragonflies spend most of their lives near the water. Adult female dragonflies lay their eggs in the water, often times attached to the stems of plants. Depending on the type of dragonfly, it can take anywhere between a few weeks to a few months for the eggs to hatch.

A newborn dragonfly is called a larva. Sometimes they are also referred to as naiads. A naiad will spend most of its life as a larva where it can live in the water for up to a few years. Naiads feed mostly on insects, such as mosquito larva, worms, and even tadpoles. Every few weeks, the dragonfly goes through a process of growth. Eventually, the naiad leaves the water where it goes through its final change and turns into a winged adult insect. Adult dragonflies usually live for a year. During this time the circle of life begins again as adult female dragonflies return to the water to release their eggs for the next batch of naiads.

1. True or False. There is more than one main idea in the passage "It's Not Easy Being Green."

   True   False

2. List the main idea(s) from the passage "It's Not Easy Being Green."

   _____

   _____

   _____

3. What is the main idea of "The Life of a Dragonfly"?
   Ⓐ Dragonflies are viewed as pests.
   Ⓑ Water pollution is destroying the habitat of the dragonfly.
   Ⓒ Amphibians can live both on land and in the water.
   Ⓓ Dragonflies go through different stages of life.

Directions: Use the Venn diagram to complete questions 4 and 5.

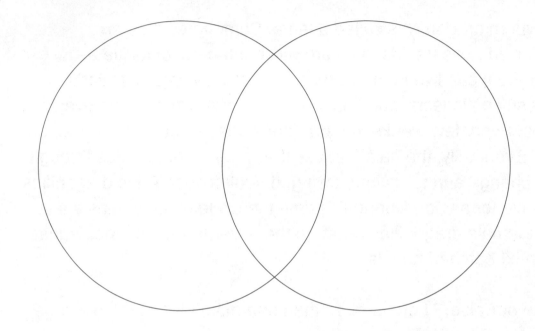

4. How are these main ideas from "It's Not Easy Being Green" and "The Life of a Dragonfly" similar?

5. How are the main ideas different?

6. What detail(s) from "It's Not Easy Being Green" supports the idea that out of the thousands of eggs that an adult frog lays only a few survive to become adult frogs?

_____

_____

_____

7. What detail(s) from "The Life of a Dragonfly" supports the idea that dragonflies live near water?

_____

_____

_____

8. Using the passage "It's Not Easy Being Green," list the three stages of a frog's life.

1.	
2.	
3.	

(Answers on pages 80–81)

DECODING WORDS

RF.3.3 Know and apply grade-level phonics and word analysis skills in decoding words.

Directions: Answer the questions below.

> To find the prefix or suffix on a word, start by finding the base word and then looking at the part that is attached at either end.

1. What is the prefix in the word **reappear**?
   How does it change the base word?

   _____

   _____

2. What is the meaning of the prefix in the word **unimpressed**?
   (A) Not   (C) Again
   (B) One   (D) Over

3. Sort the following words in the chart below to identify if they have a prefix, suffix, or no affix.

   restate   sunshine   constantly
   table   nonsense   happier

Prefix	Suffix	No Affix

4. What does the word **sadly** mean in the following sentence:

   Sadly, I will miss going to the concert.

   (A) Being full of sad   (C) The state of sadness
   (B) Feeling of sadness   (D) Without sadness

5. What does the word **amusement** mean in the following sentence?

The play had a great deal of **amusement** to it.

Ⓐ The act of being amused 　Ⓒ Full of amuse

Ⓑ The state of amuse 　　　Ⓓ Without amuse

6. What is the suffix in the word **calmness**? What does the word **calmness** mean?

_____

_____

7. How should the word **interrupt** be broken into syllables?

Ⓐ in/terr/upt 　　Ⓒ in/ter/rupt

Ⓑ i/nter/upt 　　Ⓓ inter/rupt

8. Break the following word into syllables and label each type of syllable.

resemble

_____

9. Break the following word into syllables and label each type of syllable.

disagreed

_____

10. Samantha broke the word **pineapple** into syllables as shown below. Was she correct? How do you know?

pi/neap/ple

_____

_____

(Answers on page 81)

OPINION PIECES

W.3.1 Write opinion pieces on topics or texts, supporting a point of view with reasons. (See Appendix A for substandards 3A, 3B, 3C, and 3D.)

You have just been selected class president of the 3rd grade. Your principal comes to you and asks you what changes to the school would you like to accomplish this year as president.

Choose one change you would like to make in your school. Write a persuasive piece sharing what change you would like to make and how this will positively impact your school.

Tips for your Writing:

• Include what change you would like to make
• State why you would like this change
• What impact would your change have on the school or students?

_____

_____

_____

_____

_____

_____

_____

_____

_____

_____

_____

_____

(See rubric on page 82)

CONVEYING AN IDEA

W.3.2 Write informative/explanatory texts to examine a topic and convey ideas and information clearly.

Think of a place you love to go or visit. What makes that place unique? Write an informative piece describing the place so that you can teach others in your class about why this place is special.

Tips for your writing:

- Provide details about what is unique or special about your place
- Explain why this is a special place
- Make sure your writing is teaching someone about your place, not telling a story

_____

_____

_____

_____

_____

_____

_____

_____

_____

_____

_____

(See rubric on page 83)

WRITING A STORY

W.3.3 Write narratives to develop real or imagined experiences or events using an effective technique, descriptive details, and clear event sequences. (See Appendix A for substandards 3A, 3B, 3C, and 3D.)

Your parents wanted to surprise you. They put you on a plane with your best friend for a surprise trip! When you landed, you and your best friend….

Write a narrative story describing what happens to you and your friend on this adventure.

Tips for your writing:

• Your story must have an *introduction* and *conclusion*
• Your events need to be written in a *sequence* (what happened first, next, last)
• You have to add details to your sentences, so readers have a picture in their minds as though they are right next to you on your adventure

_____

_____

_____

_____

_____

_____

_____

_____

_____

(See rubric on page 84)

GRAMMAR AND USAGE

L.3.1 Demonstrate command of the conventions of standard English grammar and usage when writing or speaking.

1. What is the relationship between a verb and an adverb?

   _____

2. What is the adjective in the sentence below?

   The speckled frog leaped across the pond.

   Ⓐ frog   Ⓒ speckled
   Ⓑ leaped   Ⓓ across

   > Most adverbs are formed by adding **ly** to an adjective.

3. What is the plural form of the noun *child*?
   Ⓐ children   Ⓒ child's
   Ⓑ childs   Ⓓ childes

4. What would you do to change the noun *box* and make it plural?
   Ⓐ Add a **-s** at the end
   Ⓑ Double the **x** and then add **-es**
   Ⓒ Add **-es** at the end
   Ⓓ Add an apostrophe (**'**) and **s** to the end of the word

5. What is the abstract noun in the sentence below?

   Happiness comes from being kind and respectful to others.

   Ⓐ being   Ⓒ respectful
   Ⓑ kind   Ⓓ happiness

6. Complete the sentence below with the correct verb.

   Yesterday in music class, we _____ our songs for the talent show.

   Ⓐ sing   Ⓒ sang
   Ⓑ singed   Ⓓ sunk

7. What is the antecedent that agrees with the pronoun in the sentence below?

   Michelle brought her new purple bike to school.

   Ⓐ Michelle   Ⓒ her
   Ⓑ brought   Ⓓ purple

8. Read the sentence below to determine the form of the adverb.

   My grandma sews better than my mom.

   Ⓐ superlative form of adverbs
   Ⓑ comparative form of adverbs
   Ⓒ positive form of adverbs
   Ⓓ linking form of adverbs

9. Complete the sentence below using a coordinating conjunction.

   Lizzette wants to buy the pizza for lunch, _____ she packed her lunch.

   Ⓐ but   Ⓒ also
   Ⓑ however   Ⓓ and

10. Write a complex sentence using the two sentences below.

    Students like to read books.
    Students' favorite books are picture books.

    Ⓐ Students read books like picture books.
    Ⓑ Students like picture books the best.
    Ⓒ Students like to read books, such as picture books.
    Ⓓ Students like picture books, but they do not like reading.

(Answers on page 85)

CAPITALIZATION, PUNCTUATION, AND SPELLING

L.3.2 Demonstrate command of the conventions of standard English capitalization, punctuation, and spelling when writing.

1. An author team is getting ready to publish their first book. They are trying to name the title of their book to send to the publisher. Using capitalization rules, you can help the authors determine the correct way to write their book title by choosing one of the following titles below:

    Ⓐ The Animals In a Jungle

    Ⓑ The Animals in a Jungle

    Ⓒ The animals in a jungle

    Ⓓ Then Animals in a jungle

2. Plain Township's fire department recently opened a new fire station. Fire Chief Snyder was writing an announcement inviting the community to attend an opening-day celebration. The announcement said: Please send your RSVP to us at 1742 Schnieder Ave, Canton, OH 44721. Help Chief Snyder to determine if the address is written correctly on the announcement, by choosing correct or incorrect.

    Ⓐ Correct

    Ⓑ Incorrect

3. Explain your answer from question 2. Why do you think the address is correct or incorrect?

    _____

    _____

4. Alexa was editing a story she wrote about going camping with her friend. In her story, she wrote:

The night sky had fallen slowly. The clouds had almost disappeared into the darkness. The temperature began to drop. Sarah's father had asked if we could bring more firewood to the fire pit, as the fire had started to fade away. Sarah and I quickly rose and dashed to the firewood. "This firewood is too heavy and dirty", I screamed. Sarah came over and helped lift the wood out of my arms. Together we carried it to the fire.

Rewrite the underlined sentence and explain what Alexa needs to do so that it is correctly written.

_____

5. Complete the following sentence by choosing the correct form of the word.

At the zoo, the _____ feathers are beautiful.
Ⓐ peacockes   Ⓒ peacock's
Ⓑ peacocks   Ⓓ peacockses

6. The _____ restroom was reserved for their use only and could not be used by the public.
Ⓐ astronauts'   Ⓒ astronautes
Ⓑ astronauts   Ⓓ astronaut's

7. What suffix would be added to the word *toast* to show past tense?
For breakfast, I toast_____ my bread.
Ⓐ -ed   Ⓒ -ly
Ⓑ -ing   Ⓓ -s

(Answers on page 86)

MEANING OF UNKNOWN WORDS

L.3.4 Determine or clarify the meaning of unknown and multiple-meaning words and phrases based on grade 3 reading and content, choosing flexibly from a range of strategies.

1. Elements help make everything around us in our world, and an element is made up of **atoms** of all one kind.

   Using the context clues, what do you think the word **atom** means?
   Ⓐ a country in our world
   Ⓑ parts that make an element
   Ⓒ items that are all the same
   Ⓓ a part of our world

2. He pointed the **telescope** toward the sky and made his first observation of the moon in space.

   Using context clues, what do you think the word **telescope** means?
   Ⓐ a long flashlight to look into small spaces
   Ⓑ a set of glasses used to look at small items
   Ⓒ an instrument used to make distant objects look larger
   Ⓓ a laser

3. People are most **contagious** during the first days of a cold, when the germs can spread easily among people.

   Using context clues, what does the word **contagious** mean?

   _____

   _____

4. The base word **sect** means *to cut*; what does the word *bisect* mean?
   Ⓐ to cut into two pieces   Ⓒ to cut with a sharp knife
   Ⓑ to cut into small pieces   Ⓓ to join together

5. The base word **struct** means *to build*; what does the word *destruction* mean?
   - Ⓐ to build very tall
   - Ⓑ to build a tower
   - Ⓒ the act of reversing or opposite of building
   - Ⓓ to build again

6. The base word **fract** means to break.
   The affix **-tion** means *expressing action or a state of being*.

   Using the base word and affix, write a definition for the word *fraction*:

   _____

   _____

7. What is the similar root word in the words below:

   realize, unreal, reality

   _____

8. Using the root word from question 7, define the word *unreal*:

   _____

   _____

9. Create a new word by using an affix with the base word *phone*.
   Then define the new word using the root word and affix.

   _____

   _____

10. How are the words *precooked* and *uncooked* different in meaning?

    _____

    _____

    _____

(Answers on pages 86–87)

FIGURATIVE LANGUAGE

L.3.5 Demonstrate an understanding of figurative language, word relationships, and nuances in word meanings.

1. Underline the simile in the sentence below. Then write an explanation of what this simile means.

   The next runner up is as fast as a fox.

   _____

   _____

2. Match the following antonyms using your knowledge of how words are related.

   _____ success   A. afraid

   _____ brave   B. joyful

   _____ angry   C. lengthy

   _____ polite   D. failure

   _____ brief   E. rude

   > *Figurative language* means words that are used in a special intentional way to suggest a meaning different from their literal definitions.

3. What is the meaning of the following simile?

   The best friends were like two peas in a pod.
   Ⓐ The best friends do everything different.
   Ⓑ The best friends both like vegetables.
   Ⓒ The best friends are very alike and close as friends.
   Ⓓ The best friends love the color green.

4. Which word has a similar meaning to **aggravated**?

  Ⓐ upset   Ⓒ funny

  Ⓑ bored   Ⓓ fast

5. Put these words in order relative to each other.

        sad   funny   hilarious   devastating

6. Replace the bold word with another word that would describe the situation in more detail.

The water **fell** from the edge of the cliff into the river below.

  Ⓐ trickled   Ⓒ whimpered

  Ⓑ shone   Ⓓ whispered

7. Which has a more positive connotation?

  Ⓐ yelled at her friend   Ⓒ grumbled at her friend

  Ⓑ talked to her friend   Ⓓ screamed at her friend

8. Find the synonym for the bold word in the sentence below.

The grass was growing at a **fast** pace from all the rain.

  Ⓐ slow   Ⓒ rapid

  Ⓑ long   Ⓓ green

(Answers on page 87)

ENGLISH LANGUAGE ARTS PRACTICE TEST

My Name: _____

Today's Date: _____

Directions: Read the passage and answer the questions below.

Cindy and the Royal Ball

Narrator: Cindy was tired of the way her stepmother and stepsisters treated her. "Do the dishes," said one stepsister, Drizella. "Clean my room," said the other, Anastasia. She was tired of all the chores. She was tired of all the jobs her stepmother gave her. In addition to all the housework, Cindy also had school and all her homework to do! Cindy was very, very tired. What she wanted was a break from all the work . . . and to have a little bit of fun.

One day, Cindy was walking home from school. She ran into one of the other girls in her class that lived on her street. Her name was Jaqueline, but was called Jaq for short.

Jaq: How-de-do, Cindy!

Narrator: Jaq always greeted Cindy the same way: "How-de-do, Cindy!" Cindy was tired of this greeting.

Jaq: What's going on?

Cindy (wearily): Nothing, I guess. Just feeling tired lately.

Jaq: Well did you hear the news?

Cindy (even more wearily): Nope. What news?

Jaq: All the kids in class were invited to a Royal Ball!

Narrator: This news caused Cindy to perk up finally.

Cindy: A Royal Ball! When?

Jaq: This Saturday. You better get dressed in your best! Didn't you receive the invitation? It came through the mail.

Narrator: Cindy shook her head from side to side.

Jaq: Well go home and check. Maybe your stepmother or stepsisters have it.

Narrator: Cindy ran home in search of the letter.

1. How would you describe Cindy's mood?
   - (A) excited
   - (B) tired
   - (C) energetic
   - (D) angry

2. In the text, next to Cindy's name it states that she is **weary**. Based on what you know about Cindy as a character, what does *weary* mean?
   - (A) Cindy doesn't like Jaq.
   - (B) Cindy doesn't want to be bothered.
   - (C) Cindy is exhausted with things in her life.
   - (D) Cindy is ready for an adventure.

3. What is the point of view of the narrator in the text?
   - (A) First person
   - (B) Third person
   - (C) Second person
   - (D) Narrative personal view

4. The narrator states "*This news caused Cindy to perk up finally.*"

   To what news was the narrator referring?
   - (A) Jaq did not greet her "How-de-do."
   - (B) Cindy got new toys.
   - (C) Cindy liked school now.
   - (D) Jaq told Cindy about a Royal Ball.

5. What does the bold word phrase mean in the following sentence?

   "This news caused Cindy to **perk up** finally."
   - (A) be kind
   - (B) be excited
   - (C) be talkative
   - (D) be annoyed

6. What is the verb in the following sentence?

   Cindy ran home in search of the letter.
   - (A) home
   - (B) letter
   - (C) Cindy
   - (D) ran

Bed in Summer

In winter I get up at night
And dress by yellow candle-light.
In summer quite the other way,
I have to go to bed by day.
I have to go to bed and see
The birds still hopping on the tree,
Or hear the grown-up people's feet
Still going past me in the street.
And does it not seem hard to you,
When all the sky is clear and blue,
And I should like so much to play,
To have to go to bed by day?

—Robert Louis Stevenson

7. How many stanzas are in this poem?

   (A) 2

   (B) 12

   (C) 13

   (D) 1

8. What is the point of view of the author in this poem?

   (A) Second person

   (B) Third person

   (C) First person

   (D) Narrative point of view

9. What can you imply about the author's bedtime from the poem?

   (A) The author stays up late

   (B) In the summer, when the author goes to bed it is light outside

   (C) The time the author goes to sleep changes in the summer

   (D) The author does not get to play in the summer

10. What does ***dress by yellow candle-light*** mean when the author states:

    In winter I get up at night
    And dress by yellow candle-light.

    Ⓐ The author does not have electricity

    Ⓑ In winter it is dark outside longer

    Ⓒ The author uses a night light to get dressed

    Ⓓ The author cannot sleep at night

11. Using the text, explain what is happening in the winter and the summer that is affecting the author's bedtime and when the author awakes.

    _____

    _____

12. Using evidence from the text, explain why it is difficult for the author to go to bed by day.

    _____

    _____

13. Justify how the last line in the poem is related to the title.

    _____

    _____

14. The author states *go to bed by day* throughout the text.

    What does the author mean by this statement?

    Ⓐ Going to bed when you want to eat

    Ⓑ Going to bed early

    Ⓒ Going to bed at a different time

    Ⓓ Going to bed when the sun is shining

Directions: Use the passage below to answer questions 15–25.

Panda Panic

The sun was starting to set when Ping reached a **fork** in the track. To the left was a path that continued alongside the river, while to the right was a path that disappeared into the forest. Which one should he take? He couldn't get lost if he followed the river, but lurking in the rock pools along its banks would be thousands of mosquitoes waiting to bite him. The forest, **on the other hand**, would be mosquito-free, but would also be darker and full of the bad sounds that Ping did not want to hear. Like that sound he was hearing now. He spun around. Behind him there was an unmistakable sound of dry leaves crunching. Ping strained every bone in his ears. There it was again. He could hear footsteps—*actual* footsteps gathering pace and running toward him!

Help! he screamed inside his head. *Please don't let it be a snow leopard!* And now that he'd had that thought, he couldn't get the picture out of his head—of sharp teeth and red eyes and hot, steamy breath in his face. There it was! There was its shadow! Spreading out from between the trees like an oozing swamp of molasses, rolling out toward him like a long, black tongue! It was huge! Ping knew that he had told his sister that he wasn't scared of snow leopards, but that was not *now*. Not now when his life was in danger. He turned and ran, his heart thumping in his chest like a war drum. He didn't look where he was going. Anywhere would do. The shadow was big and getting bigger. This was no ordinary snow leopard; this was a *giant* snow leopard that would gobble Ping up like a pistachio nut!

"NOOOOOOOOOOOOO!" he cried as the cold shadow clipped his heels and tripped him up. "LEAVE ME BE!"

"Why?" said a familiar voice behind him. "I thought I was your friend."

Ping was lying on the ground with his face in a puddle of slime. He lifted his head, turned around, and was surprised to see Little Bear standing over him.

"You again!" he exclaimed, wiping the green goo off his forehead.

15. In the first paragraph of the passage, the author states *Ping reached a fork in the track.*

    What does the author mean by the word **fork**?

    (A) Something you eat with

    (B) A bump in a track

    (C) A place where a path splits into different directions

    (D) A tool he used while on his hike

16. In the first paragraph, Ping had to make a decision.

    What was the decision he had to make?

    (A) He had to determine if he was going to follow the river or go through the forest.

    (B) He was deciding if he would wait to see the snow leopard or run.

    (C) He had to determine what the footsteps are behind him.

    (D) He had to decide if he was going to hide from the noises.

17. In the passage, the author uses the word *unmistakable.*

    What is the prefix in the word *unmistakable?*

    (A) *le*   (C) open syllable

    (B) *able*   (D) *un*

18. In the passage, the author uses the phrase *on the other hand*.
    What does the author mean by this phrase?

    (A) Ping has two hands.

    (B) Ping needs to use his other hand to count the choices.

    (C) There are both positive and negative points to the choice that Ping makes.

    (D) Ping is in need of help.

19. Circle True or False:

Ping saw a snow leopard.

True   **False**

20. Justify your answer above, using evidence from the text.

_____

_____

_____

21. Did Ping decide which path to follow?

Use evidence from the text to justify your thinking.

_____

_____

_____

22. What are Ping's current feelings about a snow leopard?

Ⓐ He told his sister he is not scared.

Ⓑ He is frightened.

Ⓒ He is confused.

Ⓓ He is excited to see one for the first time.

23. Did Ping's feelings about snow leopards change?

Explain your reasoning.

_____

_____

_____

24. How does the illustration reflect Ping's feelings when he hears the sound of the snow leopard?

Ⓐ The illustration shows he is scared when he begins to see its shadow.

Ⓑ The illustration shows that he is hiding behind the tall grass, anxiously waiting.

Ⓒ The illustration shows that he is surprised to find that it is not a snow leopard.

Ⓓ The illustration shows that he is lost by the river.

25. How did Ping's feelings about forest sounds contribute to events in the passage?

Ⓐ He didn't go to the forest because of the sounds.

Ⓑ He heard a sound and ran. Therefore, he did not choose a path to the forest or the river.

Ⓒ He told his sister the truth about snow leopards.

Ⓓ The snow leopard tripped him and gobbled him up like a pistachio nut.

Directions: Read the passage and answer the questions.
(Excerpt taken from *What's the Point of Being Green?* discussing climate change and its effects)

Help! What Can We Do?

Bad though it sounds, we can do something about it, as long as we start doing it now and the whole world gets involved—every one of us, from governments and politicians to you and me.

Scientists say that if we can limit the temperature increase to a **maximum of 3.6°F (2°C)** (a rise that they feel is already unavoidable), we may be able to escape the worst effects of climate change—although by no means all of them.

It won't be easy. It will mean altering the way we live and the way we think about our world. In fact, it will mean that we need to be **more green**! What does that mean? Well, it can mean different things to different people, but in a general way it means being aware of the environment and the impact we have on it, and doing our best to live in a way that helps rather than harms our planet.

What Are We Doing to the Climate?

To understand how Earth's climate is changing, it's useful to know a little bit about how it works. Global climate is affected by all sorts of things—the amount of energy (heat and light) coming from the Sun (solar radiation), the **atmosphere** surrounding Earth, and the ways in which the Sun's energy, the atmosphere, and Earth's surface act together.

It's All in the Atmosphere

The only reason we can live on Earth at all is because of its atmosphere. Without it, our planet would be just a dry, lifeless rock spinning in space.

The atmosphere is a mixture of gases, dust, and water droplets. These form a barrier around the planet that blocks out most of the Sun's harmful rays but allows some of its heat and light to pass through.

The Sun's heat warms up the surface of Earth, which then acts like a gigantic radiator by sending heat back into the atmosphere. Some of this surface heat escapes through the atmosphere into space, and some is held in, warming up the air closest to the surface and adding more warmth to the surface itself.

Living in a Greenhouse

This process is known as the **greenhouse effect** because it works like a greenhouse by holding in heat and smoothing out, or lessening, the extremes of hot and cold that happen between day and night.

26. What text structure do the sections *Help! What Can We Do?* and *What Are We Doing to the Climate?* represent?
    - (A) Problem and Solution
    - (B) Cause and Effect
    - (C) Description
    - (D) Question and Answer

27. What is the atmosphere?

    _____

    _____

28. What does the author tell us we can do to help the climate change?

    _____

    _____

29. What does the expression *we need to be **more green*** mean in the passage?
    - (A) We need to wear the color green.
    - (B) We need to care for the Earth.
    - (C) We need to eat more green vegetables.
    - (D) We need to grow green grass.

30. How is our planet like a greenhouse?

    _____

    _____

31. List three factors that affect our global climate:

_____

_____

_____

32. In which section from the passage would the following information best fit?

We can help our Earth by driving our cars less. When we drive our cars, harmful gases can affect our atmosphere so driving less will help reduce these harmful gases.

Ⓐ Help! What Can We Do?

Ⓑ What Are We Doing to the Climate?

Ⓒ It's All in the Atmosphere

Ⓓ Living in a Greenhouse

33. Complete the graphic organizer to tell the problem from the passage.

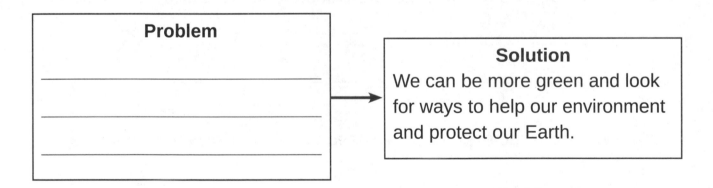

Problem
_____
_____
_____

Solution
We can be more green and look for ways to help our environment and protect our Earth.

34. How is the word *atmosphere* correctly broken into syllables?

Ⓐ at/mosph/ere

Ⓒ at/mo/sphere

Ⓑ a/tmos/phere

Ⓓ atmo/sphere

35. *The Sun's heat warms up the surface of Earth, which then acts like a gigantic radiator by sending heat back into the atmosphere.*

Which detail from the above sentence helps the reader understand what *radiator* means?

(A) the Sun's heat

(B) sending heat back into the atmosphere

(C) surface of the Earth

(D) acts like a gigantic

36. Does the author of this passage care about the Earth? How can you tell?

Support your thinking with a detail from the text.

_____

_____

_____

37. *It will mean **altering** the way we live and the way we think about our world.*

What is a synonym for the word *altering* as it is used in the sentence above?

(A) changing   (C) growing

(B) ruining   (D) discovering

38. List one way you can help our Earth based on what you read in the passage.

_____

_____

The Wind and the Sun

One day, the Wind and the Sun got into an argument. "I'm much stronger than you," said the Sun.

"Oh, really?" said the Wind. "I can bend tall trees. I can scream and howl and make all sorts of racket. You just sit there, with that goofy smile of yours. You can't move anything. You don't make any noise."

"Well then, let's have a contest," said the Sun, "that will decide who is truly stronger." At that moment, a man wearing a coat was walking along a country road.

"Okay, here are the rules," continued the Sun. "Whichever one of us can get that coat off that man is the strongest."

"Fair enough," said the Wind.

"You go first," said the Sun. The Sun politely ducked behind a cloud and the Wind began to blow. She huffed and she puffed. The man simply pulled his coat closer around him. So the Wind began to howl, causing dust to swirl and twigs to fly. But the man pulled his coat around him tighter still.

"My turn," said the Sun. The Sun came out from behind the cloud. He beamed down on the man. He covered the man in light, bathed him in warmth. The man smiled up at the Sun, happy that the cold, harsh Wind had died down. It was even getting rather hot walking along this country road. So the man took off his coat.

The Sun turned to the Wind. "Watch and learn, old friend," said the Sun. "Watch and learn."

39. What genre of story is *The Wind and the Sun*?

   Ⓐ realistic fiction   Ⓒ nonfiction

   Ⓑ fable   Ⓓ biography

40. What is the moral of this story?

_____

_____

41. What character trait describes the Sun in this story?

   Ⓐ bossy   Ⓒ harsh

   Ⓑ kind   Ⓓ sneaky

42. Use the graphic organizer below to state a character trait of the Wind and a detail to support your thinking.

Character Trait	Detail from the Text

43. *"My turn," said the Sun. The Sun came out from behind the cloud. He beamed down on the man. He covered the man in light, bathed him in warmth.*

What is an example of figurative language from the above sentences in the passage?

_____

_____

44. Why did the man take off his coat for the Sun?

   Ⓐ The man got warm from the Sun and then took his coat off.

   Ⓑ The man saw the Sun smile at him and decided to take his coat off.

   Ⓒ The man spilled his drink on his coat so he took it off.

   Ⓓ The man's coat was blown off by the Wind.

45. Why did the Wind and the Sun have a contest?

_____

_____

46. Put these events from the story in sequential order using the numbers 1–5.

_____ The Wind and the Sun decide to have a contest to see who is stronger.

_____ The Sun beams down on the man.

_____ The Sun tells the Wind to "Watch and learn."

_____ The Wind blows on the man to get him to take off his coat.

_____ The man gets warm and takes his coat off on his walk.

47. Why was the man happy that the Sun had come out?
Ⓐ He loved summer and the Sun made him think of summer.
Ⓑ He was glad that the harsh Wind had stopped and was glad to be getting warm.
Ⓒ He wanted to get a suntan.
Ⓓ He didn't like the Sun.

48. What suffix is on the word **politely**? How does this suffix change the meaning of the word?

_____

_____

49. How should the word **argument** be broken into syllables?
Ⓐ argu/ment   Ⓒ ar/gu/ment
Ⓑ arg/um/ent   Ⓓ ar/gu/me/nt

50. How do you think The Wind feels at the end of the story?
Ⓐ proud   Ⓒ humbled
Ⓑ excited   Ⓓ bored

(Answers on pages 88–91)

ENGLISH LANGUAGE ARTS ANSWERS EXPLAINED

READING: LITERATURE

Understanding Text (RL.3.1), pages 2–5

1. **B** Use the first paragraph of the passage to infer what "The Change" is that the mice are experiencing. The author writes that the mice realized they could now understand humans, and he continues on to write about two mice that want to explore their surroundings to learn more information.

2. **C** Use the information from the passage to find why Brownback is convinced to let Grayson explore the post office with Cheddar. Brownback changes his mind when Grayson suggests taking Cheddar and states that Cheddar is cautious and that "caution keeps a mouse alive." Therefore, choose answer C because Brownback lets Grayson go with Cheddar because of his cautiousness.

3. Describe Cheddar's feelings as worried, scared, fearful, or concerned (there are several other synonyms for these feelings). Support the specified feeling with a detail from the text. The final portion of the passage shows Cheddar's feelings about exploring the post office. Include support for the described feeling with the detail that Cheddar shows his surprise and shock at what he has agreed to and then compares the current situation to being scarier than the time "Grayson talked me into helping him use a pencil to trip a trap."

4. Cheddar and Grayson are exploring the post office because they can now understand humans and they want to find out more information about the post office and what happens there to share with their colony of mice. They can gain this information throughout the passage as Grayson tries to convince his father to let them go out exploring. Grayson gives reasons to his father to let them go and these can be used to explain why they are going exploring.

5. **A** Use the details at the end of this passage to make a prediction about the next event to occur in the story. At the end of the passage, Cheddar is sharing his emotions about getting involved in going with Grayson to explore and his worry and fear about what he has gotten into. Based on these details, you should predict that next Grayson and Cheddar will leave to explore the post office.

6. **B** Use the context clues to determine that the author is trying to hint what it was the panda found to use as a surfboard. The author describes the object as a perfect piece of wood that is painted green. Ping then notices that the door is missing from the ranger's office when he tries to knock on it. Therefore, you should infer that the missing door is actually the piece of green wood that is found right outside of the office.

7. **C** Use the text to locate the paragraph where Ping describes why his surfing experience did not go well the last time. Ping states, "he'd done a lot of thinking about what went wrong… it was all the fault of the surfboard—not its rider." This states that Ping believes it was the surfboard that made the experience not go well.

8. The main idea is Ping wants to try surfing again and find a better surfboard with which to try.

9. Ping thinks a single piece of wood will be flexible and able to withstand the pressure of the surfer better. Read the passage to find the details that compare Ping's previous surfboard to what he wants to use this time, which is a big piece of wood. These detail sentences explain that Ping thinks the big piece of wood will be more flexible and able to support him as he surfs.

71

10. Use the knowledge gained to write a related question about Ping, surfing, or the ranger. Questions could include: Will Ping be any better at surfing with the big piece of wood? Will the ranger come find him to get his door back? The questions should match the main idea of the section and should be related to events that could predict what will happen, or questions about events that have happened.

Fables, Folktales, and Myths (RL.3.2), pages 6–7

1. **(2)** The crow gets an idea and drops a pebble into the pitcher. **(4)** The crow keeps dropping pebbles until he can finally drink the water. Use the events in the fable *The Crow and the Pitcher* to complete the sequence chart. Use the given events to determine what happened between the crow trying to drink the water unsuccessfully and the water starting to rise. Then write the last event that happened in the story after the water started to rise.

2. **C** Read through the fable to find the problem that the crow had in the story. The fable does tell that it was a hot day and that the crow was thirsty; however, the main problem was that he could not drink the water in the pitcher because the water level was too low. Choice D is only partially correct because the crow was thirsty, but there was water in the pitcher, just too low for him to drink at first.

3. Explain that the lesson in this story is that working slowly or one step at a time pays off in the end. The crow dropped the pebbles in one by one and worked very slowly, little by little, but eventually he got what he was working for and was able to drink the water. When reading the fable, you should be looking for a lesson or moral that is being taught through the animal's actions.

4. **A** The detail that the crow continued dropping pebbles one by one for a long time supports the idea that he was working little by little toward his goal even though it was taking a long time.

5. **A** Reflect on the main idea of the fable and choose an appropriate title for this story. The main idea of the fable is related to the crow being able to get the water by dropping pebbles into the pitcher. The title *Pebble by Pebble* is related to the slow process that the crow uses to get to the water.

Characters (RL.3.3), pages 8–11

1. **A** Larry's character in the passage suggests that he is not responsible. This character trait is indicated through the text that he did not pay his cable bill and the bill is late. In the text, the author described Larry as unorganized and messy. Larry's character traits from the text indicate that he is not responsible.

2. **D** Larry describes his problem of paying the cable bill by making excuses and blaming it on his bad day. However, the narrator of the story indicates that Larry was stretching the truth. The text also indicates that Larry was unorganized, so you can infer that due to his lack of organizational skills, he did not forget or misplace a bill.

3. **A** The narrator describes Larry's character as a slob. The narrator indicates that Larry is very messy, to the point that you cannot tell if he is living in his apartment, packing to move, or just moved in.

4. Explicitly describe, yes or no; use evidence from the text that indicates why you feel you do or do not want to be Larry's friend. Use character traits to justify your reasoning. It is important to use evidence when supporting your reasons.

5. **C** In the passage, Reginald indicates that there is more to being a guard than just the keys and flashlight. It is through Reginald's advice that Larry knows he needed to take Cecil's words seriously. In the text, Reginald said "there's a little more to it than that, son."

6. **B** Cecil is very caring. He tries to give Larry detailed instructions and advice so that Larry can do the job correctly, without any surprises. Cecil continues to give Larry tips and hints about the job. "Do them all. Do them in order. Do them quick. And the most important thing to remember is don't let anything in...or out." This evidence supports Cecil's character traits in the passage.

7. **A** You can infer that Larry will have difficulties following instructions. When he was given directions from colleagues, he did not take their advice seriously. In the text, he said "Guys, come on. I can walk around an empty museum holding a flashlight." He was not taking the opportunity to listen to the other guards for advice and important information.

8. No, he fell asleep and did not read the manual. Therefore, he did not listen to their advice or instructions.

9. **D** Cecil told Larry to complete all instructions, do them in order, and do them quick. Larry wouldn't know the instructions because he fell asleep instead of reading them. Larry also did not get the instructions completed, because he was sleeping.

10. **A** Cecil would be disappointed. Cecil tried to help Larry make good choices in the passages. However, Larry did not take Cecil's advice and read the manual.

The Meaning of Words and Phrases (RL.3.4), pages 12–13

1. Describe that this phrase refers to being "filled" in a nonliteral way with a feeling of awe. Use the context clues to determine that "filled with awe" refers to having a feeling of amazement and surprise at what they were seeing. Use the second sentence, which shows that the character was questioning how these machines could be made and indicates that the character is surprised by the machines and their motion. Determine the meaning of unknown words or phrases using the surrounding context in the passage to use as clues for the unknown word or phrase.

2. **A** The nonliteral expression "scaring the fur off me" refers to being very frightened by something. You should use your understanding of figurative language to choose choice A because the mouse is referring to an expression where he would be so scared his fur would fly off of him in surprise and shock. Though this could not actually happen, the expression shows that the mouse was very scared.

3. The second sentence states that they "drove the mail to all the homes and businesses," describing what the carriers do on their job. Since the carriers left for their route, and the second sentence describes their job, then their route must be the driving that they do between the homes and businesses.

4. The mouse compares his ability to sense cheese to a TV broadcast that sends out a frequency. Look for the comparison between the two items in both sentences. The mouse states that he can sense the presence of cheese, which "sends out a frequency, like a TV broadcast." The word *like* is used to show the comparison.

5. **B** Look for context clues that help you know what the unknown phrase "caught our breath" means. This is a nonliteral phrase that can be interpreted using the previous sentence. The character scurried under the door after their friend, which signifies that they are hurrying to catch up with their friend, and then after hurrying, they would need to rest to catch their breath and let their breathing slow down.

6. The detail about the "torn rubber trim" on the door indicates that rickety describes the worn out door. Since the door has torn parts to it, then rickety must mean that something is old and worn out.

Story Vocabulary and Order (RL.3.5), pages 14–15

1. **A** This analogy compares a stanza in a poem to a paragraph in a story. A stanza in a poem is a group of lines that form a verse in a poem. It is important to refer to a stanza quickly, similarly to referring to a paragraph in

a text. Identifying stanzas quickly is important to not only find information, but also to provide evidence of points being made.

2. **B** An author often uses chapters to organize text by providing information in a logical order so the reader can best understand what they are reading. A chapter contains information that is about similar context, events, problems, and solution. Chapters help the reader to follow a story in a way that makes sense. An individual chapter may provide some new insight into a particular character or changes in the setting, but that is not the objective of the entire chapter. A chapter is a feature to help the reader to best understand a text in a logical order that follows the sequence of the story.

3. **D** Line breaks are used in a poem to provide the reader the opportunity to understand meaning through words and thoughts expressed in a poem. An author can create line breaks to highlight or signify something that is important in the poem. Line breaks are not meant to use expression. They highlight/ signify important aspects the author wants the reader to know about or understand. Line breaks are not provided to give the reader the opportunity to read fluently or take extra breaths.

4. **False:** When writing a fiction story the author uses each section of the story to build upon the previous sections to help the reader understand the events. If an author described the solution to the story and then the characters, the reader would have a difficult time understanding who is in the story.

5. If you read about the solution to the problem without knowing who is in the story, it would be confusing for the reader. When you are reading a story it is important to know who is in the story in order to understand what is happening to the characters and organize the events in your head. Authors tell about the background information including characters, setting, and problems first in the story to help them build on these parts as they write the action and solutions in their story.

6. **D** A stanza is grouped by a number of lines that are together. A stanza is separated by a

space. In this poem there are 4 stanzas. They look similar to paragraphs.

7. Use the first and second stanza to build an understanding about what others think of the boy, as he grows up. Others around him know that he does not lie, he tells the truth, and he is honest. Therefore, as a young adult or teenager, he continues to be honest and truthful. This characteristic remains constant throughout the entire poem. The stanzas are written in a succession; therefore they are similar to a timeline of the boy's life. The last stanza is referring to the boy as an adult that continues to never tell a lie.

Point of View (RL.3.6), pages 16–17

1. **B** When thinking about the point of view of text, *first person* means that the story is told by one of the characters. Often when a text is in first person, the following words are used: I, me, my, mine, we, us, our.

2. **A** The story's point of view is the perspective from which the story is written or told. A story can be written in first person or third person. The first-person point of view is when a story is told by one of the characters. The third-person point of view is when someone that is not in the story tells the story.

3. **C** The passage is written in the first person. In the passage, the character is telling the story. The character is telling the story through his perspective using "I" throughout the text. This signifies first person.

4. **B** The narrator of the passage is a cat. The narrator is speaking in first person throughout the story. The reader can infer that it is not choice D, because in the passage it "states a big man woke me up." Therefore, a big man is not telling the story. The answer is not choice A, because the texts says "his mother wouldn't let me in" so therefore the narrator is not the mother. The reader can infer that a young boy or girl found the cat and took it home. If a child found the cat, then they are not the one speaking in first person in the story.

5. **A** In the passage, the character does not have a home. This problem influences how the story is being told from the narrator's point

of view. This point of view influences readers. Readers must make a decision to either agree or disagree with how the narrator feels in the story and distinguish their own point of view. The fact that the narrator does not have a home influences readers; this problem can either impact readers to feel bad for the cat, or impact readers to agree with the other characters in the story about the cat.

6. **A** The narrator in the story feels lonely. The reader can determine this by using the text to understand the cat's feelings. The text states "I miss curling up in my chair. I miss my home . . . I crept away and hid." Then the text states, "I was so happy someone wanted me." The reader can identify the cat's feelings as loneliness, because it was excited to be wanted.

7. Use text evidence to determine your feelings about the cat. Share feelings about the cat and state why you feel a certain way based on the text. It is important that the feelings relate back to the text and not to personal experiences. An example response may be, the author makes me feel sadness for the cat. I feel this way because the cat was shaken out of a box and people continued to chase the cat away. This is sad because the cat did not have any place to go. The cat probably did not feel safe or warm at night.

8. **B** The mother does not know that the cat used to live in a home. This may change her point of view when the young boy brings the cat into the house. The mother stated that she did not want to have a smelly cat in the house. If she knew that it used to be a house cat, she may have let it in.

9. **A** In the passage the reader learns about the character and its problems through the narrator of the story. The narrator is telling the story about what has happened to the cat and its feelings. The reader does not learn or have insight from the pizza man or the boxes' point of view. The reader learns about a young child (boy) finding the cat. However, the story does not provide insight on this character's point of view. The text states "his mother" not my mother.

Text Illustrations (RL.3.7), pages 18–21

1. **C** The illustrations of a text provide the reader with a deeper understanding of the meaning of a text and set the mood of the text. The illustrations help the reader to best understand what is being said in the text through visual meaning.

2. **C** The answer is choice C because the illustration shows the characters with smiles on their faces. They look very happy and excited. The characters are running, as if they were eager to find something or someone. The text indicates they were looking for their grandfather, not playing a game or catching animals.

3. **D** *Vibrant* means lively, exciting, and energetic. Colors are often used to display character attributes in an illustration. The color choice can also be an indicator of characters and events in a text.

4. **D** His father thinks his paintings are meaningless. This can be inferred by looking at the illustration. His father's facial expression looks as if he is embarrassed, ashamed, or confused about his son's passion for painting. His father's expression on his face shows that he thinks his son's paintings are unimportant. The other responses A, B, and C would indicate that his father likes his paintings and thinks they are unique, but significant.

5. **A** The rounded shapes in this illustration indicate that the characters have a sense of comfort and happiness. These shapes allow the reader to see that the characters feel safe and loved. The rounded pictures create a bigger picture of a bouquet of flowers, which indicates the characters that are smaller in the picture are happy, content, and feel comfortable in what is occurring in the story.

6. **C** In the illustration, the artist is trying to convey that he met the love of his life. There was a beautiful woman who magically passed by. The illustration is not describing that he was lost, but that he was a painter as he was carrying a painting. The illustration

was not demonstrating that the man was using his imagination. This can be confirmed by using the text.

7. The illustration shows Papa Chagall's feelings towards Bella because in the illustration, the characters are floating towards each other as if meeting for the first time was magical. This emphasizes the text. In the text, it states "I saw a girl standing on a bridge." "As soon as I saw her, I knew that Bella was the one for me."

8. The colors of the illustrations in a text help to determine the mood the author is trying to set. If the illustrator uses dark colors, they may be trying to show danger or a character being scared or frightened. If an illustrator uses light colors in the picture, they may be trying to show safety or calmness. If an illustrator uses contrasting colors that make something stand out, they may be trying to bring the reader's attention to something in the illustration.

9. **A** The illustration shows the characters flying in the air with flowers in her (Bella's) hands. The illustration shows that the characters are happy and delightful. The reader can infer that they are married. The answer is not choice B, because the reader must think about what the characters look like in the illustration. They do not look upset or scared. The answer is not choice D, because if Papa Chagall got a new painting job, the reader should think about what would be in the illustration to show he got a new job. For the answer to be choice C, the flying would not be symbolic, and would be to give an indication of where Papa Chagall and Bella were going.

READING: INFORMATIONAL TEXT

Understanding Text (RI.3.1), pages 22–23

1. **C** Use the text to answer this literal question, which asks where the Stellar sea lions live. Answers to comprehension questions are found within the details in the story.

2. **False.** The information in the text states that "adult males weigh between 1,300 and 2,500 pounds" and "females weigh about 1,000 pounds."

3. **C** The first sentence of the paragraph answers this question as it refers to the Northern sea lion and directly states that it is also known as the Stellar sea lion.

4. Problems affecting the Northern sea lion: being hunted for their fur, being hunted for food, habitats being affected by pollution, their food source, fish, is being threatened due to overfishing. Use the second paragraph of the text to find the information that states the various problems affecting the Northern sea lions.

5. **B** The information about the countries that hunt seals is in the first paragraph of the text. This question asks to name the country that is *not* listed in the paragraph, so think carefully to match up the countries listed with those in the answer choices. The United States of America is not listed as a country that allows seal hunting, therefore seals are not hunted there.

6. Seals are hunted for their pelts, blubber, meat, and bones. List two of these reasons on the lines provided. Use the text to find the detail which lists why seals are hunted in order to answer this question. Make sure to refer to the text when answering this question rather than using any of your prior knowledge.

7. Countries set quotas so that the seals do not become endangered because too many of them are being killed. Use the information in paragraph 2 in order to determine why these quotas are set in these countries. Determine the meaning of "quota" as the overall number of seals to be killed and then use the author's detail that "quotas are used to make sure that people do not excessively overhunt seals and cause the populations to become endangered" to answer this question.

Main Idea and Details (RI.3.2), pages 24–25

1. **C** Find the main idea by reading the entire passage and looking for details throughout the passage that support one main idea. In this passage note that the details all relate to the idea that cats have not changed a great deal over time and still have many qualities of their wild ancestors.

2. Describe how the main idea of a passage is found by looking through the entire passage to find the central idea that is related to all the supporting details. This passage includes details about cats and their characteristics that help them survive and how these characteristics have existed in the species throughout time.

3. Details could include: Cats are good hunters and use their senses to help them hunt. Cats have strong senses of sight and hearing that help them hunt. Cats can use their whiskers as radar to help them sense things around them. Find details within the passage that support the main idea that cats have changed very little over time from their wild ancestors.

4. The main idea of this passage is that cats have changed very little over time from their wild ancestors. Therefore, the supporting details should also be related to how the cats are similar to their ancestors and the traits that they have that help them survive and hunt.

5. **A** Find an alternate title by using the main idea of the passage and choosing a title that relays the same main idea. The main idea of this passage relates to how cats have changed very little from their ancestors. This main characteristic is their ability to hunt and the qualities they have that make them a good hunter.

6. **C** Use the details in the story to find the answer to this question. In the third paragraph the author compares the cat's whiskers to radar in its ability to sense objects around itself.

7. Cats can rely on their senses of sight, hearing, and touch to help them hunt. This information can be found throughout the details in the passage. The article shares that cats use their sense of touch using their whiskers as a tool to guide them in the night when they are hunting. Cats use their sense of hearing because they have better hearing than dogs or humans and can use their ears to hear tiny sounds to help them hunt. Cats also are able to detect small movements even out of the corner of their eyes in order to spot prey as they are hunting.

Relationships Between Texts (RI.3.3), pages 26–27

1. Describe how both passages discuss the brain's purpose for communication. "On the Job" explains that the brain instructs other parts of the body on what they should do in response by communicating body functions. "Right Down the Middle" discusses how the different hemispheres of the brain communicate and control different parts of the body.

2. The passages describe the brain's functions and how it works. "On the Job" provides an understanding of the purposes of the brain. The passage "Right Down the Middle" describes how the brain works under the skull to control the left and right side of the body.

3. All of the passages are about the brain. Look for similar main ideas among the three passages and similar content/words that are used throughout the writing to determine how they are related.

4. "It's All in Your Head"—This section describes how your body protects your brain within the skull.

5. "Right Down the Middle"—This section describes how your brain is composed of two parts.

6. The author included these sentences as an introduction about what the passage will be about. These sentences provide a few big ideas about the detailed information within each section of the passage. When an

77

author writes a nonfiction piece it is important that he or she gives us the background knowledge we need to understand the information that is presented.

7. Look for a set of events in which one event caused the second to occur. In this section, it describes that the body can respond, therefore this response is an effect. The student should then look at the information provided to determine what causes the body to have a response.

   Cause: The brain processes information received from the world around you.

   Effect: The brain instructs the parts of the body on what to do in response.

Text Features and Search Tools (RI.3.5), pages 28–29

1. **C** The table of contents is a tool to help the reader determine what information is in a nonfiction book as well as where it is located within the text. The table of contents is a text feature that is located at the beginning of a work. It often outlines the main topics that are discussed in a particular text.

2. **B** The index is a text feature that provides a list of key words and topics in a book and the pages on which each term can be found. The topics in an index are usually listed in alphabetical order. The index does not have definitions of words. The index is always in the back of a book.

3. **A** A search box helps a reader find information efficiently because it allows the reader to type in what they are looking for, and then the website generates all topics related to the word or words typed.

4. **B** A hyperlink cannot be used in a book that is not digital. A hyperlink is a tool that can only be implemented digitally. A hyperlink is used to help connect to new information. A hyperlink is used in a digital text. This can be through an ebook, digital newspaper or magazine, digital project (such as PowerPoint), or Internet site. Not every digital text or tool contains a hyperlink.

5. **True.** An icon can be either a picture or a word that when clicked takes the reader to a location with new information. An icon can also be used to help better understand a word or idea that is confusing in a text. For example, if you are reading about an animal and you do not know what it looks like or anything about its habitat, there may be an icon you can click on to gain this information.

6. Nonfiction text has features that makes it easier to locate information quickly. These features help you know how a text is organized and how to use the whole of, or part of, a text to gain new knowledge.

7. **D** A subheading gives the reader information about key topics in a particular section of the text that can be found under a heading. A heading lists the key topics in a text. If a subheading is present, then it is underneath a heading. A subheading provides more specific information under the heading within the text.

8. **A** In a nonfiction text, an author often puts into bold type words that maybe unknown to the reader. These words can be defined either in the text or in another part of the book. If a book has a glossary, these bold words are often found there, at the end of a book, with a definition. The definition helps the reader to understand what the word means.

Point of View (RI.3.6), pages 30–31

1. **A** A point of view is the author's view or position on a subject. When writing, an author shares ideas and/or thinking by writing to inform, persuade, entertain, or share. Therefore, the point of view isn't the opinion the author is using to persuade the reader, but rather the information the author provides by explaining their thinking, ideas, or understanding of a topic.

2. **B** The author is providing an opinion on why wetlands are important. This allows the reader to determine the author's point of view because it clarifies the position that wetlands are in danger, and they provide important resources. The word "important"

indicates how the author feels about wetlands but does not provide factual information about the topic. There are additional sentences in the passage that provide facts. For example, *"Wetlands have also been damaged by pesticides used on farms, chemicals used in factories, and oil spills at sea."* This statement is a fact about how wetlands have been damaged, but when it is isolated it does not provide insight into the author's point of view. Therefore, in this passage, the word *important* supports the author's opinion about the topic.

3. **B** The author's point of view is that wetlands are important and need to be saved. The author states: *Wetlands are also an important resource, providing food, building materials, and other products that people need and use every day. However, this important ecosystem is in trouble.*

4. **C** When reading a text, it is important to build an understanding of the words the author is using to describe their point of view to determine when the author is providing facts and/or an opinion. In the passage, the statement *"Wetlands are also an important resource…"* shows how the author feels about wetlands. The word important indicates that the author cares about wetlands and is trying to inform readers about their significance.

5. You can either agree or disagree with the author. If you agree, than you need to use the text to determine why you agree. What about the text do you identify with? If you disagree with the author, than use the text to justify why you disagree. What knowledge do you have on the subject that may provide a different insight? What evidence or facts were missing that would have helped you find a connection to agree with the author's point of view? Did the author's message help you make connections to the world or other texts?

6. Use evidence in the text by indicating part of the passage that helped you formulate your point of view. If you agree or disagree, you still must be able to use the text to determine your reasoning. If you indicate that a personal experience or prior knowledge influenced your viewpoint, you must link these back to the text. For example, if going to visit a park reminded you of a wetland, link a piece of the passage into the experience at the park in order to distinguish your point of view from that of the author's.

7. No, it is important to know that when reading a text you can agree or disagree with the author. Your opinion, knowledge, and experiences may influence your understanding and awareness about what the author is teaching, which will distinguish your own point of view.

Making Connections (RI.3.8), pages 32–33

1. **A** It is important to understand that a comparison text tells about two different items or topics and mentions the similarities and differences. A Venn diagram allows you to list the qualities for each topic independently, and in the inner portion list the similarities between the topics.

2. **Compare and Contrast.** You need to choose compare and contrast because this structure takes two or more topics and lists aspects that are the same (compare) and different (contrast) about these topics.

3. **Question and Answer.** Choose question and answer because in this text structure, a question is posed, and then answered in the following sentences to provide information about a topic.

4. **Sequential.** Choose sequential here because items in a sequence are presented in chronological (time) or numerical order. These could include listing steps to follow or events that occur in a day or time period.

5. **Cause and Effect.** Choose cause and effect in this case because this text structure lists an event that is the cause of another occurrence (effect or result). A cause-and-effect relationship looks at two events and how they are related to each other.

6. **Description.** Choose description because this text structure describes, or gives information about, a topic to inform the reader.

7. **Problem and Solution.** The answer is problem and solution because this text structure presents a problem and then describes one or more solutions to the problem. The solution presents a way to fix the problem that is occurring.

8. **D**, Cause and Effect; **A**, Sequence; **C**, Comparison; **E**, Description; **B**, Question and Answer; **F**, Problem and Solution

   Use the given knowledge of text structures to match the examples of the structure to the type. These text structures exist in short and longer passages and help readers understand the purpose of the writing and the information presented.

9. **D** It is important to know that a sequential text structure tells events in a chronological or numerical order. The key word *finally* signals an order and tells the last event in a series. The other listed key words do not relate to a sequence or order of events.

10. **B** You should have an understanding that a compare and contrast text structure tells the similarities and differences between two or more topics. Therefore, the key words *a similarity* would be used to indicate characteristics that are the same between the topics.

Compare and Contrast (RI.3.9), pages 34–37

1. **False.** There can be just one main idea in a passage and this main idea can be found by using the supporting details, finding a central theme, and using the title as a tool. The main idea in this passage is that there are many difficult circumstances that a frog faces throughout its years of development.

2. The main idea of the passage is that frogs face many difficult struggles in their life, which makes their life not an easy one to survive. Use the title as a tool to determine the main idea. Read the passage looking for a central idea that the details relate to in order to find the main idea.

3. **D** Determine the main idea of this passage by using the title as a tool and then finding the central idea that the details in the passage all support. This passage outlines the phases of life that a dragonfly goes through as it grows, therefore answer D accurately tells the main idea of this story.

4. Use the inner portion of the Venn diagram to describe the ways in which these two stories are similar. This could include: both passages describe the life of an animal, both passages share how the animal changes over time, both passages tell about the different phases that the animals go through in their life. Use the information from questions 1–3 to compare the main ideas of the two passages. Think about the central ideas in both passages and what they have in common.

5. Use the outer portions of the Venn diagram to contrast the two main ideas. "It's Not Easy Being Green" is different because it is about the struggles that a frog must survive in order to become a frog. "The Life of a Dragonfly" is different because it is about the different phases of the dragonfly and how they become a winged insect.

6. In the first paragraph the author tells that other animals will eat many of the eggs. This detail supports the idea that only a few of the thousands of eggs grow to be adult frogs. Another detail that supports this idea occurs later in the article when the author states that other animals eat the tadpoles before they are able to grow into an adult frog. Find the details that show the struggles that keep the eggs from surviving in order to support this idea.

7. Adult dragonflies lay their eggs in the water, often attached to plants. The first phase of a dragonfly's life is as larva where it spends a few years in the water. These details support why a dragonfly is often found near the water. Look in the text to find details that tell why the dragonfly is near the water in order to support this idea.

8. 1. Egg Stage
    2. Larva or Tadpole Stage
    3. Adult Frog Stage

    Use the details in the article to find the phases of the frog's life. The article is organized in a sequential order that moves through the life of a frog. Therefore, find the first phase at the beginning of the article and continue to move through the article to find the second and third stages.

READING: FOUNDATIONAL SKILLS

Decoding Words (RF.3.3), pages 38–39

1. The prefix is re-; this changes the base word appear. Re- means to do again; therefore, reappear means to appear again.

2. **A** The prefix in the word *unimpressed* is un-. This prefix means not; therefore the word *unimpressed* means you are not impressed.

3. Use your knowledge of affixes in order to identify the base or root word and find if there are any affixes added to the word in order to sort it into the correct column. You should identify commonly used prefixes and suffixes in the words in order to sort them accurately.

Prefix	Suffix	No Affix
restate	constantly	table
nonsense	happier	sunshine

4. **B** You should recognize the suffix -ly as meaning a feeling of or characteristic of; therefore sadly would mean a feeling of sadness.

5. **A** The suffix -ment means the act or process of; therefore amusement in the sentence refers to the act of being amused by the play.

6. The suffix is -ness, and the word *calmness* means a state of being calm because the suffix -ness has the meaning of a state of.

7. **C** The first syllable must have a consonant at the end to make a closed syllable, the second syllable will have the r-controlled/er/ without the double r, and the final syllable will include the doubled letter "r" and the closed syllable.

8. re/sem/ble: *re-* open, *sem-* closed, *ble-* consonant-le. You should hear that there are 3 syllables and then look for the vowel sounds as a tool for helping them split the word. The first syllable has the long e sound; therefore it must be an open syllable.

9. dis/a/greed: *dis-* closed, *a-* open, *greed-* vowel team/pair.

10. Samantha is not correct. She did break the word into 3 syllables, which is the correct number of syllables and she tried to find a pattern to make the long *i* sound in the first syllable. However, the word *pineapple* should be split: pine/ap/ple.

81

WRITING

Opinion Pieces (W.3.1), pages 40–41

	3	2	1
Opinion Statement	Introduces the topic using a clear and concise opinion statement.	Uses an opinion statement that is not clearly identified to the reader or at the beginning of the opinion piece.	Does not use an opinion statement to identify point of view.
Reasons	Provides multiple reasons that strongly support the opinion and persuades readers towards the writer's point of view.	Provides limited reasons that support the opinion and do not clearly persuade the reader toward the writer's point of view.	Provides one or no reason that supports the opinion.
Linking Words and Phrases	Uses a variety of linking words and phrases to connect the opinion statements and reasons. e.g., *because, therefore, since, for example*	Uses limited linking words and phrases that do not clearly connect the opinion statements and reasons.	Does not use linking words and phrases to connect the opinion statements and reasons.
Organization	Uses an organized structure in the opinion piece to introduce an opinion, support the opinion with reasons, and provides a concluding statement.	Inconsistently uses an organized structure in the opinion piece to introduce an opinion, support the opinion with reasons, and provides a concluding statement.	Does not use an organized structure in the opinion piece to introduce an opinion, support the opinion with reasons, and provides a concluding statement.
Concluding Statement	Ends the opinion piece using a clear and concise concluding statement.	Uses a concluding statement that is not clearly identified, or is not at the end of the opinion piece.	Does not use a concluding statement in their opinion piece.
Spelling	Uses grade-level phonics and high-frequency-word skills to accurately spell words within the piece.	Inconsistently uses grade-level phonics and high-frequency-word skills to accurately spell words within the piece.	Does not use grade-level phonics and high-frequency-word skills to accurately spell words within the piece.
Mechanics: punctuation, capitalization, grammar	Uses grade-level-appropriate capitalization, punctuation, and grammar skills to create a writing piece that can be read fluently.	Inconsistently uses grade-level-appropriate capitalization, punctuation, and grammar skills to create a writing piece that can be read fluently.	Does not use grade-level-appropriate capitalization, punctuation, and grammar skills to create a writing piece that can be read fluently.

Conveying an Idea (W.3.2), pages 42–43

	3	2	1
Introduction	Introduces the topic in a clear and concise way.	Introduces the topic, but it is not clearly identified to the reader.	Does not introduce the topic.
Text Features	Uses facts, definitions, and details to support and describe the topic.	Does not use all text features (facts, definitions, and details) to support and describe the topic.	Uses only one or no text feature (facts, definitions, and details) to support and describe the topic.
Linking Words and Phrases	Uses a variety of linking words and phrases to connect ideas within categories of information. e.g., *also*, *another*, *and*, *more*, *but*	Uses limited linking words and phrases that do not clearly connect ideas within categories of information.	Does not use linking words and phrases to connect ideas within categories of information.
Organization	Uses an organized structure in the informational piece to group information into like sections to make it easier to learn about the topic.	Inconsistently uses an organized structure in the informational piece to group information into like sections to make it easier to learn about the topic.	Does not use an organized structure in the informational piece to group information into like sections to make it easier to learn about the topic.
Concluding Statement	Ends the informational piece using a clear and concise concluding statement.	Uses a concluding statement that is not clearly identified, or is not at the end of the informational piece.	Does not use a concluding statement in the informational piece.
Spelling	Uses grade-level phonics and high-frequency-word skills to accurately spell words within the piece.	Inconsistently uses grade-level phonics and high-frequency-word skills to accurately spell words within the piece.	Does not use grade-level phonics and high-frequency-word skills to accurately spell words within the piece.
Mechanics: punctuation, capitalization, grammar	Uses grade-level-appropriate capitalization, punctuation, and grammar skills to create a writing piece that can be read fluently.	Inconsistently uses grade-level-appropriate capitalization, punctuation, and grammar skills to create a writing piece that can be read fluently.	Does not use grade-level-appropriate capitalization, punctuation, and grammar skills to create a writing piece that can be read fluently.

	3	2	1
Introduction	Introduces the characters and establishes the situation for the narrative writing piece.	Only introduces one of the following—the characters or the situation—for the narrative writing piece.	Does not introduce the characters or establish the situation for the narrative writing piece.
Reasons	Uses dialogue and descriptions to develop experiences and events. Could include: *character descriptions, actions, thoughts, feelings, or reactions to the situation*	Uses dialogue or descriptions to develop experiences and events.	Does not use dialogue or descriptions to develop experiences and events.
Temporal Words and Phrases	Uses temporal words or phrases to signal event order. e.g., *first, next*	Uses limited temporal words or phrases to signal event order.	Does not use temporal words or phrases to signal event order.
Organization	Uses an organized structure in the narrative piece that allows the story to unfold naturally.	Uses an organized structure in the narrative piece but this structure does not allow the story to unfold naturally.	Does not use an organized structure in the narrative piece.
Closure	Provides a sense of closure to the narrative piece.	Concludes the story without resolving all situations and events.	Does not conclude the story.
Spelling	Uses grade-level phonics and high-frequency-word skills to accurately spell words within the piece.	Inconsistently uses grade-level phonics and high-frequency-word skills to accurately spell words within the piece.	Does not use grade-level phonics and high-frequency-word skills to accurately spell words within the piece.
Mechanics: punctuation, capitalization, grammar	Uses grade-level appropriate capitalization, punctuation, and grammar skills to create a writing piece that can be read fluently.	Inconsistently uses grade-level appropriate capitalization, punctuation, and grammar skills to create a writing piece that can be read fluently.	Does not use grade-level appropriate capitalization, punctuation, and grammar skills to create a writing piece that can be read fluently.

LANGUAGE

Grammar and Usage (L.3.1), pages 46–47

1. An adverb modifies a verb. Therefore, it clarifies the meaning of the verb by giving further explanation or detail. An adverb answers any of the following questions about a verb: *how*, *when*, *where*, and *why*. For example, *Mark climbed the ladder slowly;* (*slowly* describes *how* he climbed) *climbed* is the verb and *slowly* is the adverb.

2. (**C**, speckled) An adjective is a word that describes a noun. A noun is a person, place, or thing. In this sentence, *speckled* describes the frog. This indicates that *frog* is the noun (thing) and *speckled* describes it.

3. **A** The plural form of the noun *child* is *children*. When making some nouns plural, you cannot add an –s or –es to the end. These types of nouns are called irregular nouns. When making an irregular noun plural, the whole word changes. For example, *child* to *children*, *mouse* to *mice*, *goose* to *geese*.

4. **C** When making a noun plural, you are referring to more than one person, place, or thing. When making the word *box* plural, you need to add an –es to the end of the word. When making most nouns plural, you add an –s. With some nouns you need to add an –es. These are nouns that typically end in ch, sh, s, x, or z, or if a noun ends with the consonant **o** as with potato-potatoes.

5. (**D**, happiness) An abstract noun is a noun that cannot be touched, heard, smelled, tasted, or seen. In this sentence, *happiness* is a thing or feeling. Although this can be classified as a thing, it cannot be touched, heard, smelled, seen, or tasted. These are often referred to as the five senses, as they are abstract.

6. (**C**, sang) The answer is *sang*. This is an irregular verb. Irregular verbs are verbs that when used in past tense do not follow the rules of using –ed at the end. Typically, when a verb is regular and is changed to past tense, you place an –ed at the end. For example, these are forms of a regular verb: I like to jump rope. Yesterday I jump*ed* rope. An irregular verb can change in each tense, such as sink, sank, sunk. Often, when verbs change to a past tense, -ed ending is added. However, with some verbs the entire word changes as the tense changes, and those are called irregular verbs.

7. (**A**, Michelle) The antecedent in the sentence is Michelle. The pronoun in the sentence is *her*. Both the pronoun and antecedent are singular, feminine, and in third person. Therefore, these two words—*Michelle* and *her*—agree.

8. **B** The sentence compares two people, therefore the sentence is in the comparative form. The verb or action is *sews*, and the sentence is concerned with who is better at it, mom or grandma. If the sentence read "My grandma sews the best in the family," it would be a superlative form of an adverb, because it compares three or more persons, places, and things.

9. (**A**, but) A conjunction connects individual words to groups of words. A coordinating conjunction connects words to words or a phrase to a phrase. In this particular sentence, the conjunction is connecting these two clauses: *Lizzette wants to buy her lunch/ She packed her lunch*. The following words are coordinating conjunctions: *and, but, for, nor, or, so, yet.* The word *and* can also be used in other instances and sentence structures.

10. **C** *Students like to read books, such as picture books*. A complex sentence has one independent clause and one dependent clause. An independent clause can stand alone as its own sentence. A dependent clause cannot stand alone, as it is not a complete thought. In the example sentence, the independent clause is *Students like to read books*. The dependent clause is *such as picture books*. When these two clauses are put together with a comma, they create a complex sentence.

Capitalization, Punctuation, and Spelling (L.3.2), pages 48–49

1. **B** When capitalizing words in a title, the first and last word is always capitalized. Additionally, nouns, pronouns, verbs, adverbs, and adjectives are capitalized in a title. In this title the words *the*, *animals*, and *jungle* need to be capitalized.

2. **A** When writing an address as a line of text, a comma is needed between the street and the city. There is no comma between letters and numbers (house number and street, and state and zip code).

3. Explain that this is correct because it is written as a line of text. Therefore, commas are needed after the street and city. When writing an address as a line of text, a comma is needed between the street and the city. There is no comma between letters and numbers (house number and street, and state and zip code). It is important to understand the difference between comma placements when an address is written in text versus across multiple lines as seen on an envelope or letter.

4. *"This firewood is too heavy and dirty," I screamed.* When rewriting this sentence, the comma needed to be moved in before the ending quotation mark. When placing a comma in quotation marks, it is used to separate a direct quote from the person speaking (*she replied* or *he said laughingly*). Periods and commas always go inside quotation marks, which helps to set apart a speaker's words.

5. **C** The answer is choice C because an apostrophe **s** ('s) indicated possession. The peacock owns the feathers. Therefore it is an apostrophe s. An apostrophe s is often added to a singular noun to show possession. If the noun is plural than an apostrophe comes after the s. If the noun is singular and ends with an s or z an apostrophe can come at the end of the word.

6. **A** The answer is choice A because the word *astronauts is plural.* The restroom is reserved for multiple astronauts. Therefore, when you are showing possessives of plural nouns, the apostrophe is added at the end of the word.

7. **A** For breakfast, I *toasted* my bread.

   When adding -ed to the end of a word, the inflection makes the word a past-tense verb.

Meaning of Unknown Words (L.3.4), pages 50–51

1. **B** Use the context clues in the sentence that describe what an atom is in relation to elements. The sentence states that "an element is made up of atoms of all one kind," therefore the student should understand that this sentence could be used to define the unknown word **atom**.

2. **C** Use the sentence to determine that the person is using a telescope to look at the moon, which is an object far away. The context of the sentence includes someone using the telescope as a tool to see the moon. Therefore, you can determine that a telescope must be used to look at objects far away, and determine the answer to be choice C.

3. Use the context of the sentence to determine that **contagious** refers to germs being spread between people, such as when you get a cold. You should describe that contagious means spreading or passing between each other. The sentence uses the context of a cold to aid students in understanding the word *contagious.*

4. **A** The student should use their knowledge of the affix **bi-** found in words such as bicycle to know that this affix refers to *two*. This affix is combined with the base word *sect* in the word **bisect**. Therefore, you can determine the meaning of the word **bisect** to refer to cutting into two pieces or parts.

5. **C** Use the knowledge of the affix **de-**, which refers to the reversal or removal, and the suffix **–tion** that is the result of doing an action. Combine these affixes with the base word **struct** to form **destruction**. *Destruction* would be defined as the act of reversal or removal of building; or destroying something.

6. A *fraction* means the result of breaking apart. The student should use the definitions to create a combined definition for the word *fraction* using the base word and affix. You can also use prior knowledge of a fraction to determine which meaning of *-tion* should be used.

7. Similar root word: *real.*

8. Use the root word **real** with the affix **un-** and define *unreal* as not true or not a fact. You should have an understanding that a root word can have varying affixes to change its meaning.

9. Responses could vary and include words such as telephone, headphone, or microphone. Then, use the root word **phone**, meaning *sound* or *an instrument used for sound,* in combination with an affix to define a new word. Example: telephone- an instrument that helps sound travel across distances.

10. The student should explain that even though both words share the base word **cook**, they differ in meaning based on their affix. The word *precook* is the act of something *being cooked before.* The word *uncooked* is the act of something that has *never been cooked or not been cooked.* The affix on these words impacts the meaning of the base word and creates different meanings.

Figurative Language (L.3.5), pages 52–53

1. You should underline *fast as a fox.* Describe that this simile is comparing the running of the person to the running of a fox. This simile lets the reader know that the runner is very fast just as a fox is very fast at running. Look for an expression that compares the subject of the sentence using "like" or "as" when trying to find a simile.

2. **D** success   A. afraid
    A brave   B. joyful
    B angry   C. lengthy
    E polite   D. failure
    C brief   E. rude

Use your knowledge of antonyms meaning words that are opposite in relationship to each other. Therefore, look to find words with opposite meanings when matching the words.

3. **C** Look for the simile in the sentence by using the words *like* or *as* to find what the best friends are being compared to. You then have to understand whether this is a literal or nonliteral comparison. You need to know that the expression *two peas in a pod* has a nonliteral meaning, expressing that the best friends are very close and alike as friends.

4. **A** Use your understanding of language and words to understand that *aggravate* is a word used when something displeases someone and that another word with a similar meaning is choice A, **upset**.

5. Devastating, Sad, Funny, Hilarious (or reverse order). Order the words using their meaning to determine how they are related in describing a state of mind. You could order the words starting with the most negative state of mind to the most positive, or from the most positive to the most negative state of mind.

6. **A** You should be looking for a word with a similar meaning to **fell**, but that more accurately describes the situation in more detail while matching the context of the sentence. You should choose answer A, because it is a verb that describes the movement of water in a detailed manner.

7. **B** You should understand comparisons of words in relation to each other and look for the phrase that shows a positive connotation. Compare the three responses to determine which is more positive. You will find that **talked** is most positive in comparison to **yelled** and **grumbled**.

8. **C** Try to find a synonym to the word **fast**; looking for a word that has a similar meaning. The word **fast** is a synonym for **rapid**.

ENGLISH LANGUAGE ARTS PRACTICE TEST, pages 56–70

1. **B** tired. Cindy's character in the beginning of the play is uninterested in her chores, school, and her friend Jaq. The text indicated that she is very tired. This would allow the reader to know that she is not excited, energetic, or angry. (RL.3.3)

2. **C** Cindy is exhausted with things in her life. The text and narrator have indicated that Cindy is tired. Another word for **tired** is **exhausted**. The narrator describes all the things that Cindy is tired of; these are things, places, and people that are a part of Cindy's life. (RL.3.1, RL.3.4, L.3.4)

3. **B** The point of view of the narrator in this text is third person. The narrator is an outside character or observer to the text. The narrator is providing insight into the characters' thoughts and feelings. (RL.3.6)

4. **D** Jaq told Cindy about a Royal Ball. This news was exciting for Cindy, and she became interested in what Jaq had to say. (RL.3.1)

5. **B** to be excited. *Perk up* means to get excited about something unexpectedly. (RL.3.4, L.3.4)

6. **D** ran. A verb is an action word. The action in the sentence is **ran**. The other choices are nouns. (RF.3.3, L.3.1)

7. **D** 1. There is one stanza in this poem. A stanza is a group of lines that are separated by a space. There is no extra space between any of the lines, so there is only one stanza in this poem. (RL.3.5)

8. **C** first person. The author in the poem is speaking about his (or her) own personal experience. The narrator of the poem used the word *I*. This word indicates first person. (RL.3.6)

9. **B** In the summer, when the author goes to bed, it is light outside. This can be inferred because the text says *in summer quite the other way; I have to go to bed by day*. This means that in the summer, the sun is still shining and it is light. (RL.3.1)

10. **B** In winter it is dark outside longer. This can be inferred from the text, when the author states *In the winter I get up at night, and dress by candle-light*. Therefore, when the author gets up in the winter, it is dark outside and there is no light, so he (or she) has to use a candle. (RL.3.4, L.3.4)

11. In the winter, the sun is not out as long. The days are shorter and the nights are longer. It is darker for longer periods in the winter. This affects the author because he (or she) does not see light in the morning when awakening and needs a candle. In the summer, the days are longer and there are more hours when the sun is shining. Therefore, when the author goes to bed, birds are still out and the sky is clear. The changing of the seasons and sun are affecting what it is like outside when the author goes to bed and wakes up in the winter and the summer. (RL.3.1, RL.3.5)

12. It is difficult for the author to go to bed by day because when he (or she) goes to bed he (or she) sees things that occur during the day. For example, the author sees birds hopping on a tree, hears people's feet outside, and says the sky is clear and blue. (RL.3.1)

13. The last line is related to the title of the poem, because the author describes going to bed by day in the summer time. The author uses the text to describe what it is like to go to bed with the sun still shining in the summer. (RL.3.1)

14. **D** going to bed when the sun is shining. The poem provides explicit examples about what it looks like and sounds like to go to bed by day. The poem does not indicate a change in bedtime, punishment, or a change in daily routines. Therefore, you should be able to infer and connect that going to bed by day means going to bed when the sun is out. (RL.3.5)

15. **C** a place where a path splits into different directions. When someone uses the term a *fork in the road* it means that there are two different directions, choices, or paths one can take. This is a form of figurative language. (RL.3.4, L.3.5)

16. **A** The decision that Ping had to make was to determine if he wanted to take the path that followed the river or the path that went into the forest. (RL.3.1)

17. **D** The prefix in the word *unmistakable* is *un-*. A prefix is a word part that comes before the root or base word. The prefix *un* means not. A suffix is a word part that comes after the root or base word. The suffix in this word is *able*, which means can do. (RF.3.3)

18. **C** There are both positive and negative points to the choice that Ping makes. The phrase *on the other hand* often refers to comparing two ideas in order to decide which is best. (RL.3.4, L.3.4)

19. **False.** The text explicitly states that he thought it was a snow leopard. As Ping was screaming *NOOO....*a familiar voice behind him said *"I thought I was your friend."* The text then states that it was Little Bear standing there. (RL.3.1)

20. The text explicitly states that he thought it was a snow leopard at first. The text then states that it was Little Bear standing there. The reader should be able to understand that Ping thought it was a snow leopard but it was not. Ping then responded to Little Bear *you again*! (RL.3.1)

21. No, he did not decide. When Ping heard footsteps and thought it was a snow leopard, the text states that he turned and ran. The text also states that he didn't look where he was going, anywhere would do. (RL.3.1, RL.3.3)

22. **B** Ping is frightened of a snow leopard. The text did state that he had told his sister that he was not scared, but that was not now. This means that he is now scared of snow leopards. Ping is not excited to see one for the first time; as the shadow crept closer to him, he turned and ran. (RL.3.1)

23. Yes, Ping's feelings about snow leopards changed. In the text, it states that he told his sister that he was not scared of snow leopards. The text then states *but that was not* now. *Not now when his life was in danger.* The text shows that Ping's feelings did change through his experience in the

passage. It can be inferred that Ping is now scared of snow leopards because of his later actions and words. (RL.3.3)

24. **A** The illustration shows that Ping is scared when he begins to see the creature's shadow. Ping's facial expression in the illustration shows that he heard something as his ears are perked up and is scared. (RL.3.7)

25. **B** He heard a sound and ran. Therefore, he did not choose a path to the forest or the river. Since Ping heard the noises, the dilemma or problem in the first part of the first paragraph was not solved. This is evidenced in the text, when the text states *he turned and ran, his heart thumping in his chest like a war drum. He didn't look where he was going. Anywhere would do.* (RL.3.3)

26. **D** Question and Answer. These sections start with a heading that poses a question, and then this question is answered in the following paragraph. Use your knowledge of text structures to understand that question/answer structures have a question that is stated and then answered in the text. (RI.3.1, RI.3.8)

27. The atmosphere is a mixture of gases, dust, and water droplets that surrounds Earth. It helps block out some of the harmful sun rays, and lets in some sun to help heat the Earth. Use the section *It's All in the Atmosphere*, as well as the bolded word **atmosphere** to find details that indicate the meaning of this unknown word. Then combine this information to provide a meaning for *the atmosphere*. (RI.3.1, L.3.4)

28. We can be more "green" by thinking about the way we live and being aware of how we are impacting our environment as we try to help the Earth, not harm it, to slow down the climate change. (RI.3.1)

29. **B** From reading the passage, you need to demonstrate an understanding of the non-literal expression *to be green* as it relates to helping and caring for the Earth. The section *Help! What Can We Do?* informs the reader that being green is about thinking how we can help the Earth and be more responsible with our environment. Look for the *green*

89

expression within the passage and use the context clues surrounding the expression to help understand its meaning. (L.3.5)

30. Our planet is like a greenhouse because the atmosphere helps hold in heat and keep the temperature changes from being too hot or too cold in the day and night. Search for this information using the heading *Living in a Greenhouse*. In this section, you use the details to determine why our planet is like a greenhouse. (RI.3.1, RI.3.7, L.3.5)

31. 1. The amount of energy that comes from the sun

    2. The atmosphere around our Earth

    3. How the atmosphere, the sun's energy, and Earth's surface interact with each other

    Use the details in the text to find reasons that impact our global climate. (RI.3.1)

32. **A** Choose a heading that matches this detail. The detail is about a way we can help our Earth, and the section *Help! What Can We Do?* provides information about ways we can be more green and help, rather than harm, our Earth. (RI.3.8)

33. The problem is that our climate is changing and the temperature is increasing in our world. Use the main idea from the passage to help write the problem. The solution is listed; therefore, you should look for a problem statement that matches the solution. (RI.3.3)

34. **C** Use your understanding of syllable types to help break apart the word *atmosphere* into syllables. You can hear the vowel **a** making its short sound in the first syllable; therefore, it must be closed. The vowel **o** is making its long sound in the second syllable; therefore, it must be open; and then the final syllable follows with "sphere." (L.3.2)

35. **B** Use the context clues from the sentence to help determine the meaning of the unknown word. The sentence uses the word *by* to connect the unknown word **radiator** to a description of what it does. Therefore, you can understand that the surface of the Earth is like a radiator because it sends heat back into the atmosphere. (L.3.4)

36. The author cares about the Earth because there is a passage telling how we need to help solve the problem of climate change. The author tells the readers how they can help our environment by making choices that are *green* to help reduce our impact on the environment. Since the author writes details about how we can make changes to help and not harm our Earth, you can determine that the author cares about the Earth. (RI.3.1)

37. **A** Understand that a synonym is a word with the same meaning as another. Look for a word that can be substituted in the sentence above and have the same meaning. The word *alter* is a synonym for the word *change*; therefore, Answer A is correct. (L.3.5)

38. Use the information in the passage to write about a way to help the environment and the Earth. These efforts could include: using less electricity, turning off the water to save water when washing hands or brushing teeth, turning off lights when leaving a room, or using less paper to help save trees. The reason should be one that would impact the environment and use fewer resources to save energy and help keep the climate from changing so quickly. (RI.3.7)

39. **B** Use your understanding of various genres and types of stories in order to determine that this story, which has the fictitious characters the Sun and the Wind, is a fable. You should know that a fable is a story that has animals or characters talking who are not able to actually speak in reality. You should also know that a fable is a story with a moral or lesson that you can learn from the characters and their actions. (RL.3.2)

40. The moral of *The Wind and The Sun* is that you do not always have to use force and bullying to get what you want. Being nice and kind can get the results you need rather than being mean. You can see that the Sun and Wind took different approaches in the contest and that the Wind was harsh and mean, whereas the Sun was kind and gentle. You can then determine that the kinder approach was the one that won the contest. (RL.3.2)

41. **B** You should determine that the Sun is kind in the story because of the gentle approach used to get the man to take off his coat. Rather than being harsh and mean, the Sun simply shines and warms the man. (RL.3.3)

42. You could describe the Wind as bossy, mean, or a bully. The character trait you choose should show that the Wind takes a more aggressive approach to the contest in comparison to the Sun. You should then support the character trait with a detail from the text. You could use the detail that the Wind huffs and puffs and then howls at the man to try to get him to take his coat off. You could also use the details from the text when the Wind describes how it can bend tall trees, scream and howl, and move things around. (RL.3.3)

43. Figurative language: *covered the man in light or bathed him in warmth.* These expressions both describe how the Sun helped warm the man and make it easy for you to picture this happening. The Sun does not actually cover up the man, but the expression suggests that the man has light all over him from the sun. Similarly, the expression *bathed him in warmth* does not refer to a literal bath, but rather conveys that the man is covered with warmth just as you are covered with water in a bath. (RL.3.4, L.3.5)

44. **A** It was getting hot along his walk from the Sun coming out so he decided to take his coat off. (RL.3.1)

45. The Wind and the Sun had a contest to decide who was stronger. They were arguing and decided to have a contest to see who could get the man to take his coat off. Use the text to go back and find the details that tell why the contest happened between the Wind and the Sun. The Sun says that the contest will prove who is really stronger. (RL.3.1, RL.3.3)

46. **1** The Wind and the Sun decide to have a contest to see who is stronger.

    3 The Sun beams down on the man.

    5 The Sun tells the Wind to "Watch and learn."

    2 The Wind blows on the man to get him to take off his coat.

    4 The man gets warm and takes his coat off on his walk.

    (RL.3.1)

47. **B** The man was happy that the Wind had stopped its harsh blowing and that instead the warm sun was out. He then started to even get hot on his walk. The student should go back into the text to answer this question by finding the event when the Sun came out and the man was happy. (RL.3.1)

48. The suffix on the word *politely* is *-ly.* This changes the word polite to mean having the characteristic of being polite. The word *politely* tells how the Sun acted; it was polite in its actions. (RF.3.3)

49. **C** The word *argument* has three syllables, therefore, look for answers with three syllables. Then use the vowel sounds to determine that the second syllable should follow an open syllable pattern in order for the u to make its long sound. Therefore, *argument* should be broken apart as ar/gu/ment. (RF.3.3)

50. **C** Infer and understand that since the Wind thought that he would easily win the contest, but then is proved wrong by the Sun, that the Wind would feel humbled. At the beginning of the story, the Wind was proud and thought that he was easily stronger, but the Wind was humbled at the end of the story to realize that being mean and harsh with the man did not win him the contest. (RL.3.1)

MATH

The Common Core mathematics standards are created to be building blocks between grade levels. The concepts learned in K–2 are foundational skills necessary for students to master grade 3 concepts. This allows teachers to make sure that achievement gaps are closed and that students have prior knowledge to continue their learning with more challenging concepts.

The Common Core standards in K–2 allow students to build strong number sense with whole numbers as they learn to count, order numbers, and compare numbers. A student's ability to think about numbers flexibly and understand the relationships between numbers is imperative to the concepts that are taught throughout all grade levels. In grade 3, students continue to have standards in Number Operations and Base Ten, Operations and Algebra, Measurement and Data, and Geometry. However, new to students in grade 3 is the standard for Number and Operations—Fractions. This is a foundational stepping stone to further learning in upcoming grade levels.

UNDERSTANDING MULTIPLICATION

> **OA.A.1** Interpret products of whole numbers, e.g., interpret 5 × 7 as the total number of objects in 5 groups of 7 objects each. *For example, describe a context in which a total number of objects can be expressed as 5 × 7.*

1. What multiplication equation would match the picture below?

Ⓐ 4 × 6   Ⓒ 3 × 4

Ⓑ 6 × 4   Ⓓ 1 × 10

2. What multiplication equation matches this repeated-addition equation?

3 + 3 + 3 + 3 + 3 + 3 + 3

Ⓐ 3 × 7   Ⓒ 7 × 3

Ⓑ 5 × 4   Ⓓ 6 × 3

> The × sign means *groups of*, and you can substitute these words when solving equations to help you picture the total.

3. What multiplication equation matches the skip counting below:

2, 4, 6, 8, 10, 12, 14

Ⓐ 7 × 2   Ⓒ 4 × 7

Ⓑ 2 × 2   Ⓓ 7 × 4

4. Represent the equation 4 × 5 using a picture, and then find the product of 4 × 5.

5. The Annual July 4th Dog Walk was taking place at the Alum Dog Trail. Cassidy was watching the dogs walking on the course. Cassidy was counting the legs on the dogs as they walked by her. She wrote the equation 9 × 4 to represent what she saw on the dog walk.

A. How many dogs did Cassidy see on the dog walk? _____

B. How many legs in all did Cassidy see? _____

6. What does the equation 4 × 8 represent?

_____

_____

7. Does this strategy represent the multiplication equation 3 × 9 = 27?

$$3 + 3 + 3 + 3 + 3 + 3 + 3 + 3 + 3 = 27$$

How do you know?

_____

_____

(Answers on page 165)

UNDERSTANDING DIVISION

> **OA.A.2** Interpret whole-number quotients of whole numbers, e.g., interpret
> 56 ÷ 8 as the number of objects in each share when 56 objects are
> partitioned equally into 8 shares, or as a number of shares when 56 objects
> are partitioned into equal shares of 8 objects each. *For example, describe
> a context in which a number of shares or a number of groups can be
> expressed as 56 ÷ 8.*

1. Six students share 24 pieces of candy equally. Using the candy pieces,
   show how they can share them equally.

   How many pieces of candy will each student get? _____

2. A class of 28 students is divided into 4 equal teams to play a game
   during recess. Model, using a picture, how the students are divided
   and write an equation to match the picture.

   > The ÷ sign means you are
   > sharing or grouping the
   > dividend. Make sure you think
   > about whether the problem is
   > sharing or grouping!

   Equation: _____

3. How are the equations below similar? How are the equations different?

   $$56 \div 8 = 7 \qquad 56 \div 7 = 8$$

   _____

   _____

   _____

4. Which division equation(s) could match this picture?

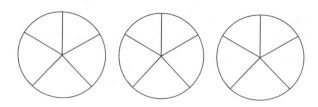

(A) $15 \div 3 = 5$

(C) $15 \div 5 = 3$

(B) $3 \div 15 = 5$

(D) $18 \div 3 = 6$

5. Using question 4, how do you know the equation(s) match the picture?

_____

_____

6. Using the space below, model the division equation $45 \div 9 =$ ____ using any strategy, then complete the equation below.

$45 \div 9 =$ _____

7. Explain how you could represent the given equation using sharing or grouping/partitioning.

$$27 \div 3 = 9$$

Sharing: _____

_____

Grouping/Partitioning: _____

_____

(Answers on pages 165–166)

SOLVING WORD PROBLEMS

> **OA.A.3** Use multiplication and division within 100 to solve word problems in situations involving equal groups, arrays, and measurement quantities, e.g., by using drawings and equations with a symbol for the unknown number to represent the problem.

1. The school cafeteria is ordering more milk for lunch. They order chocolate milk in containers of 12 cartons each. If they order 5 containers of milk, how many cartons will they have to sell in the cafeteria? Show your work using pictures, numbers, and words.

> If you are stuck, draw your picture first to help you visualize what is happening.

2. The playground is painting new hopscotch squares for the kindergarten students. If each hopscotch board has 8 squares and they want to paint 5 new boards, how many squares will they need to paint? Show your work with pictures, numbers, and words.

3. Beth and Calla decide to share a chocolate bar between them. They unwrap the chocolate bar to find that it has 3 rows of 4 chocolate pieces. How many chocolate pieces are there in the chocolate bar? Show your work with pictures, numbers, and words.

4. Using your work from problem 3, if Beth and Calla share the chocolate bar equally, how many chocolate pieces will they each get? Show your work with pictures, numbers, and words.

5. A baker is making chocolate chip cookies to sell in his shop. He mixes up the chocolate chip cookie dough batter and wants to bake 24 cookies at a time on a cookie sheet. How could he arrange the cookies into equal rows to bake in the oven? Show your work with pictures, numbers, and words.

6. Alex bought candy hearts to pass out to his classmates in gift bags. He opened the bag of candy hearts and found out that there were 54 candy hearts. If he splits this bag of hearts equally into 6 gift bags for his friends, how many candy hearts should he put in each bag? Show your work with pictures, numbers, and words.

7. The 8th grade marching band was getting ready for the annual 4th of July parade. The band director asked them to line up in rows of 4 students per row so that they would fit down the street. If there are 36 members in the band how many rows will there be of students marching in the parade? Show your work with pictures, numbers, and words.

(Answers on pages 166–167)

DETERMINE UNKNOWN NUMBERS

> **OA.A.4** Determine the unknown whole number in a multiplication or division equation relating three whole numbers. *For example, determine the unknown number that makes the equation true in each of the equations* $8 \times ? = 48$, $5 = \_\_ \div 3$, $6 \times 6 = ?$

1. Which number makes this equation true? $4 \times 6 = \_\_\_\_\_$

   (A) 24   (B) 12   (C) 10   (D) 30

2. Which number makes this equation true? $\_\_\_\_\_ \times 2 = 18$

   (A) 7   (B) 36   (C) 9   (D) 10

3. Which number makes this equation true? $30 = \_\_\_\_\_ \times 6$

   (A) 180   (B) 5   (C) 15   (D) 9

4. Which number makes this equation true? $7 \times \_\_\_\_\_ = 28$
   Explain your strategy for solving.

   _____

   _____

5. Which number makes this equation true? $8 \times \_\_\_\_\_ = 48$
   How can the equation $48 \div 6 = 8$ help you find the missing factor?

   _____

   _____

   _____

6. Which number makes this equation true? $45 \div 5 = \_\_\_\_\_$

   (A) 7   (B) 10   (C) 9   (D) 6

7. Which number makes this equation true? _____ $\div 3 = 9$

   (A) 3

   (B) 27

   (C) 12

   (D) 36

8. Which number makes this equation true?

   $42 \div$ _____ $= 6$

   (A) 10

   (B) 6

   (C) 7

   (D) 48

REMEMBER

The = sign means *the same as*. Work to find the missing numbers and make the two sides of the equation equal.

9. Which number makes this equation true? _____ $\div 4 = 8$
   How does the multiplication equation $8 \times 4 = 32$ help you find the missing dividend?

   _____

   _____

   _____

10. Complete the following multiplication and division equations using the given numbers:

    3, 21, 7

    _____ $\times$ _____ $=$ _____   _____ $\div$ _____ $=$ _____

    _____ $\times$ _____ $=$ _____   _____ $\div$ _____ $=$ _____

(Answers on pages 167–168)

PROPERTIES OF OPERATIONS FOR MULTIPLICATION AND DIVISION

OA.B.5 Apply properties of operations as strategies to multiply and divide. Examples: If $6 \times 4 = 24$ is known, then $4 \times 6 = 24$ is also known. (*Commutative property of multiplication.*) $3 \times 5 \times 2$ can be found by $3 \times 5 = 15$, then $15 \times 2 = 30$, or by $5 \times 2 = 10$, then $3 \times 10 = 30$. (*Associative property of multiplication.*) Knowing that $8 \times 5 = 40$ and $8 \times 2 = 16$, one can find 8×7 as $8 \times (5 + 2) = (8 \times 5) + (8 \times 2) = 40 + 16 = 56$. (*Distributive property.*)

1. Which equations show an example of the commutative property of multiplication?

   Ⓐ $6 \times 2 = 12$ and $2 \times 6 = 12$

   Ⓑ $9 \times 2 = 18$ and $3 \times 6 = 18$

   Ⓒ $3 \times 2 \times 2 = 12$ and $6 \times 2 = 12$

   Ⓓ $8 \times 1 = 8$ and $3 \times 7 = 21$

   > The properties of operations are the rules that you can use to help you solve equations.

2. Use 2 multiplication strategies to model the commutative property for the equations 7×3 and 3×7.

   _____

   _____

   _____

   _____

3. Model using the distributive property to solve this equation:

   $8 \times 6 =$ _____

   _____

   _____

   _____

   _____

4. Match the following equations with the property of multiplication they represent.

A. $5 \times 4 \times 6 =$ _____
   $5 \times 4 = 20$ Distributive Property
   $20 \times 6 = 120$

B. $7 \times 6 = 42$ Associative Property
   $6 \times 7 = 42$

C. $8 \times 2 = 16$
   $8 \times 5 = 40$ Commutative Property
   so, $8 \times 7 = 8 \times (5 + 2) = 56$

5. Sarah was solving the equation 9×7 but couldn't remember her 9s facts. She knew her 5s facts really well and knew that $9 \times 5 = 45$. What other fact can Sarah use to help her solve out 9×7? Show your thinking below.

_____

_____

_____

6. Model using the associative property to solve this equation:

$$6 \times 5 \times 2 = \underline{\quad}$$

_____

_____

7. Which of the following properties is represented by the following equations:

$$8 \times 9 = (8 \times 5) + (8 \times 4) = 40 + 32 = 72$$

Ⓐ Commutative Property
Ⓑ Distributive Property
Ⓒ Associative Property

Explain how you know _____

_____

(Answers on pages 168–169)

DIVISION: UNKNOWN FACTORS

OA.B.6 Understand division as an unknown-factor problem. *For example, find 32 ÷ 8 by finding the number that makes 32 when multiplied by 8.*

1. Match the following multiplication equations to the related division equations.

   Ⓐ $7 \times 6 = 42$
   Ⓑ $8 \times 4 = 32$
   Ⓒ $4 \times 4 = 16$
   Ⓓ $9 \times 2 = 18$

   1. _____ $16 \div 4 = 4$
   2. _____ $32 \div 8 = 4$
   3. _____ $18 \div 2 = 9$
   4. _____ $42 \div 6 = 7$

   > *Inverse* means the opposite. Addition and subtraction are inverse operations just as division and multiplication are inverse operations. Think about why this makes sense.

2. How can the multiplication equation $8 \times 6 = 48$ help you solve the equation $48 \div 8 =$ _____?

   _____

   _____

   _____

   _____

3. How can the equation _____ $\times 5 = 30$ help you solve $30 \div 5 =$ _____? What is the missing number to make the equations true?

   _____

   _____

   _____

   _____

4–6. Complete the given chart by writing the related multiplication equation to match the division equation.

Multiplication Equation	Division Equation
4.	$63 \div 9 = 7$
5.	$56 \div 7 = 8$
6.	$20 \div 4 = 5$

7–9. Complete the given chart by writing the related division equation to match the multiplication equation.

Multiplication Equation	Division Equation
$3 \times 6 = 18$	**7.**
$7 \times 5 = 35$	**8.**
$4 \times 6 = 24$	**9.**

10. How are multiplication and division related? Explain your thinking.

_____

_____

_____

(Answers on page 169)

SOLVING TWO-STEP WORD PROBLEMS

> **OA.D.8** Solve two-step word problems using the four operations. Represent these problems using equations with a letter standing for the unknown quantity. Assess the reasonableness of answers using mental computation and estimation strategies including rounding.

1. Mr. Jones was setting up tables in the cafeteria for a celebration lunch for the 3rd grade students. The school owned 75 chairs and they were borrowing 48 more chairs from the middle school. If there are 120 people attending the celebration lunch, are there enough chairs for everyone? If not, how many more chairs do they need; if there are enough, how many extra seats are there? Show your work with pictures, numbers, and words.

_____

_____

_____

_____

2. Adam and John went to the book fair to buy some new books for the summer. John spent $8 on a new superhero novel. Adam spent 3 times as much as John on a detective kit. How much more did Adam spend than John at the book fair? Show your work with pictures, numbers, and words.

> Make sure to check: Does my answer make sense?

_____

_____

_____

_____

3. Nora really wants to get a puppy and her parents told her if she could save enough money she can get the puppy. Nora decides to start saving $5 of her allowance each week. On Nora's birthday her grandma gave her $20 to help her save for the puppy, too. If she has been saving for 10 weeks, how much money does Nora have so far for her puppy? Show your work.

_____

_____

_____

_____

4. Karla went to the store to buy some gum to share with her friends after school. She bought 6 packs of strawberry bubble gum. Each pack has 4 pieces of gum. If she shares the gum with her and 4 friends, how many pieces can they each get? Will there be any left over? Show your work with pictures, numbers, and words.

_____

_____

_____

_____

5. The 3rd graders decide to plant a garden on the playground to study plants. They plant sunflowers that need 8 ounces of water each day to grow. They also planted lettuce that needs 6 ounces of water each day to grow. How much water do they need to water their plants for a week? Show your work.

_____

_____

_____

_____

6. Kirk's mom gives him $50 to spend at the pool in June. It costs $4 for admission to the pool for the day and Kirk likes to buy a snack at the snack bar each day, too. He buys a popsicle to help him stay cool when he goes to the pool and it costs $2. How many days can Kirk go to the pool and get a popsicle until his money runs out? Show your work with pictures, numbers, and words.

_____

_____

_____

_____

7. At the end of year field day the school orders pizza for the students to eat for lunch. They can order a large pizza with 8 slices or an extra-large with 12 slices. If they need 68 pieces of pizza for the 3rd grade students, how many of each size of pizza should they order so that there are no left overs? Show your work with pictures, numbers, and words.

_____

_____

_____

_____

8. The Possum Hill Elementary School was doing a penny-war drive to raise money for the local animal shelter. On Monday, the 2nd graders brought in 228 pennies and the 3rd graders brought in 415 pennies. On Tuesday, the 2nd graders brought in 524 pennies and the 3rd graders brought in 407 pennies. Who brought in more pennies so far? Which set of equations will help you estimate the answer?

Ⓐ 228 + 524 = _____ and 415 + 407 = _____

Ⓑ 300 + 500 = _____ and 400 + 400 = _____

Ⓒ 200 + 500 = _____ and 400 + 400 = _____

Ⓓ 300 + 600 = _____ and 500 + 500 = _____

9. Who brought in the most pennies? Show your work.

_____

_____

10. The Coleman family went on a trip to Colorado to go camping at Rocky Mountain National Park. They stopped along their way for lunch after driving 178 miles. After enjoying lunch, Mr. Coleman said that it was time to head out and they got back in the car. They stopped for gas after another 103 miles. When they got back in the car, Mrs. Coleman said they were not stopping again until they got to the hotel, which was 276 miles away. If they wanted to travel 500 miles, did they meet their goal? How many miles have they traveled on their first day of driving?

_____

_____

_____

_____

(Answers on pages 170–171)

ARITHMETIC PATTERNS

OA.D.9 Identify arithmetic patterns (including patterns in the addition table or multiplication table) and explain them using properties of operations. *For example, observe that 4 times a number is always even, and explain why 4 times a number can be decomposed into two equal addends.*

1. Holly was looking at her addition table during Math class and noticed that when she looked diagonally the digits were the same in that line. She looked at the equations that made a sum of 9: 0 + 9, 1 + 8, 2 + 7, 3 + 6, 4 + 5, 5 + 4, 6 + 3, 7 + 2, 8 + 1, and 9 + 0. What pattern exists in these equations? How do we know we have written all the equations that have a sum of 9? Show your thinking.

_____

_____

2. If you multiply any integer by 2, the product will always be an even number. Explain using numbers and words if this statement is true or false.

An integer is any whole number that is not a fraction.

_____

_____

3. Kirk is solving the equation 7 × 4. He says he can solve this by solving 7 × 2 and then doubling the product. Is this true? How do you know? Show your thinking.

_____

_____

_____

4. Complete the input/output table using the given rule.

Input	Output
25	
14	
9	

Rule: − 6

Input	Output
16	
10	
8	

Rule: Divide by 2

Input	Output
6	
4	
3	

Rule: × 3

5. Find the rule for this input/output table. Explain how you know.

Input	Output
24	6
12	3
8	2

Rule: _____

_____

_____

_____

6. Complete the input/output table and find the rule.

Input	Output
4	12
	3
9	
3	9

Rule: _____

7. If you know 7 × 10 = 70, how can you use that to help you solve the equation 7 × 9? Explain your thinking with numbers and words.

_____

_____

8. If you know that 2 × 8 = 16, how can you use doubling to help you solve 8 × 8? Explain your thinking with numbers and words.

_____

_____

(Answers on pages 171–172)

ROUNDING WHOLE NUMBERS

NBT.A.1 Use place-value understanding to round whole numbers to the nearest 10 or 100.

1. When rounding to the nearest ten, what number does 834 round to?

   Ⓐ 800 　　　Ⓑ 840 　　　Ⓒ 835 　　　Ⓓ 830

2. When rounding to the nearest hundred, what number would 852 round to?

   Ⓐ 900 　　　Ⓑ 850 　　　Ⓒ 800 　　　Ⓓ 1000

3. Write 2 numbers that would round to 340 when rounded to the nearest 10.

   Make sure to determine which place value you are rounding to!

   A. _____ and _____

   B. Explain, how did you know that these numbers would round to the nearest 10?

   _____

   _____

4. Which of the following rounds the number accurately?

   Ⓐ 2367 when rounded to the nearest 10 is 2365

   Ⓑ 4569 when rounded to the nearest 100 is 4600

   Ⓒ 3687 when rounded to the nearest 10 is 3680

   Ⓓ 4382 when rounded to the nearest 100 is 4300

5. Place an ✗ on the number line below where the number 783 would be located.

   ←——————————————————————→
   750　　　　　　　　　　　　　　　800

6. Place an **X** on the number line below where the number 352 would be located.

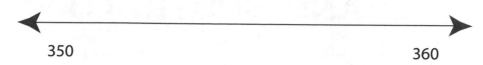

350   360

7. The post office needs to hire a new mail carrier to help deliver mail for the shift that delivers the most mail. They want the new mail carrier to work either the Thursday and Friday shift or the Monday and Tuesday shift. On Monday there were 346 pieces of mail delivered. On Tuesday there were 621 pieces of mail delivered. On Thursday there were 212 pieces of mail delivered. On Friday there were 627 pieces of mail delivered. Rounding to the nearest 100, which shift should the new mail carrier work? Explain your thinking.

_____

_____

_____

8. While playing a board game, Sam rolled three dice that made 643 as the largest number. Erin rolled three dice and her number was 629. Erin thinks that Sam's and her number when rounded to the nearest 100 are the same. Do you agree or disagree with her thinking? Justify your reasoning.

_____

_____

_____

_____

(Answers on pages 172–173)

FLUENTLY ADD
AND SUBTRACT

NBT.A.2 Fluently add and subtract within 1000 using strategies and algorithms based on place value, properties of operations, and/or the relationship between addition and subtraction.

1. Using place value, complete the following number sentence.

$$462 + 334$$

The solution is: _____

> When you are fluently adding and subtracting numbers, consider each number's place and its value, using relationships you know to compose and decompose numbers.

2. Using words, justify how you used place value to solve the problem above.

_____

_____

3. How can you use addition to solve this problem, 690 − 568? Explain your reasoning below.

_____

_____

4. What equation represents the following story problem. There *from* − are 48 people in line to ride Speedster the roller coaster, <u>and</u> + 128 people in line for bumper cars. How many more people are in line for bumper cars than Speedster?

Ⓐ 48 + 128

Ⓑ 128 − 48

Ⓒ 48 − 128

Ⓓ None of the above

5. What is the solution to 782 + 216.

The solution is: _____

6. Justify, in words, how you used number relationships to solve the problem in question 5.

_____

_____

_____

7. Rationalize how you can use number relationships to solve 700 − 698.

_____

_____

_____

_____

8. Which of the following number sentences is true?
Ⓐ 206 + 508 = 114 + 600
Ⓑ 206 + 508 = 714 + 2
Ⓒ 200 + 514 = 700 + 4
Ⓓ 506 + 212 = 14 + 700

9. Which equation shows the associative property of addition?
Ⓐ 10 + 8 + 2 = 11 + 7 + 2
Ⓑ (8 +2) + 3 = 8 + (2 + 3)
Ⓒ 12 + 7 = 7 + 12
Ⓓ None of the above

(Answers on pages 173–174)

MULTIPLES OF TEN

NBT.A.3 Multiply one-digit whole numbers by multiples of 10 in the range
10–90 (e.g., 9 × 80, 5 × 60) using strategies based on place value and
properties of operations.

1. Using place-value blocks, draw a model to solve 4 × 10.

> *Place value* tells the value of each
> digit in a number. For instance,
> 132 has 1 group of 100, 3 groups
> of 10, and 2 groups of 1.

4 × 10 = _____

2. Find the solution: 10 × 7 = _____
    Ⓐ 40   Ⓑ 7   Ⓒ 700   Ⓓ 70

3. Find the solution: 9 × 10 = _____
    Ⓐ 900   Ⓑ 90   Ⓒ 70   Ⓓ 9

4. Explain how you can find the solution to 8 × 10.

    _____

    _____

5. Model below, using pictures or words, how you can solve
    the equation:

    6 × 40 = _____

    _____

    _____

6. How are these equations similar?

$$3 \times 70 = \underline{\hspace{1cm}} \qquad 3 \times 7 \times 10 = \underline{\hspace{1.5cm}}$$

_____

_____

_____

7. Find the solution: $60 \times 9 = \underline{\hspace{1.5cm}}$

Ⓒ 600   Ⓓ 54   Ⓔ 240   Ⓕ 540

8. Find the solution: $7 \times 70 = \underline{\hspace{1.5cm}}$

Ⓒ 490   Ⓓ 49   Ⓔ 350   Ⓕ 400

9. Lucy went to the store to buy fruit snacks for her class. She bought 6 packs of fruit snacks. Each pack had 10 fruit snacks inside. How many fruit snacks does she have to give out to her class? Show your solution using an equation and words/pictures to show your strategy.

_____

_____

_____

10. The 3rd graders were going on a field trip and needed buses to drive them. There are 4 classes of 3rd graders at Pine Elementary and each class has 30 students. How many students will need to travel on the buses to the field trip? Show your solution using an equation and words/pictures to show your strategy.

_____

_____

_____

(Answers on pages 174–175)

BUILDING AN UNDERSTANDING OF FRACTIONS

NF.A.1 Understand a fraction 1/*b* as the quantity formed by 1 part when a whole is partitioned into *b* equal parts; understand a fraction *a/b* as the quantity formed by *a* parts of size 1/*b*.

1.

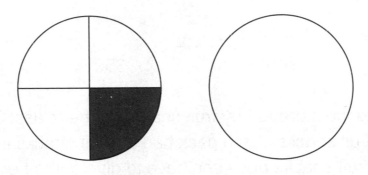

A. How many parts does it take to fill the whole in the partitioned circle?

_____

B. What fraction is represented by the shaded part?

_____

2. Split the shape below into 4 equal parts, shade $\frac{1}{4}$ of the whole.

3. How many $\frac{1}{4}$ pieces would you need to make $\frac{3}{4}$? How do you know?

_____

4. Split the shape below into 8 equal pieces.

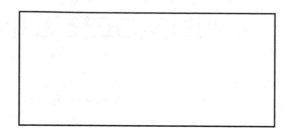

Shade in $\dfrac{6}{8}$ of the whole rectangle.

How did you know what to shade?

_____

5. What does the 3 represent in the fraction $\dfrac{1}{3}$?

_____

6. What does the 6 represent in $\dfrac{1}{6}$?

_____

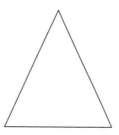

7. Split the shape above into 2 equal parts, shade $\dfrac{1}{2}$ of the whole.

_____

_____

(Answers on pages 175–176)

FRACTIONS ON
A NUMBER LINE

NF.A.2 Understand a fraction as a number on the number line; represent fractions on a number-line diagram. (Also see Appendix for 2a and 2b.)

1.

0   1

Divide the number line to show the fraction $\frac{1}{4}$, and then label $\frac{1}{4}$ on the number line.

2. How did you know where to divide your number line and label the fraction $\frac{1}{4}$?

_____

_____

3.

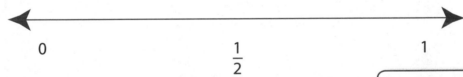

0                          $\frac{1}{2}$ 1

Which fraction is closest to $\frac{1}{2}$?

(A) $\frac{1}{3}$ (B) $\frac{1}{4}$ (C) $\frac{1}{10}$ (D) $\frac{1}{1}$

> Fractions always represent sharing into equal parts. When you compare fractions, make sure to look at the size of the fractional parts and the number of parts labeled with the numerator.

4. Using the number line, label the fractions $\frac{1}{8}$, $\frac{2}{8}$, $\frac{3}{8}$, $\frac{4}{8}$, $\frac{5}{8}$, $\frac{6}{8}$, $\frac{7}{8}$, $\frac{8}{8}$.

0   1

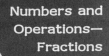

5. How did you know where to label the fraction $\frac{5}{8}$?

_____

_____

6.

Using the fraction $\frac{1}{3}$ on the number line, iterate the fraction to make the whole. Label each of the fractions that you iterate.

7.

Using the fraction $\frac{1}{4}$ on the number line, iterate the fraction to make the whole. Label each of the fractions that you iterate.

8. Is the fraction $\frac{5}{6}$ closer to 0, $\frac{1}{8}$, $\frac{1}{2}$, or 1?

Ⓐ 0   Ⓑ $\frac{1}{8}$ Ⓒ $\frac{1}{2}$ Ⓓ 1

9.

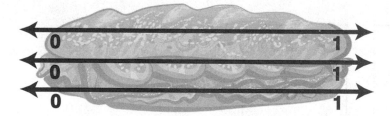

Ella, Lucy, and Evan went to the sub shop for lunch. They each got their own sub to enjoy together. Ella ate $\frac{3}{8}$ of her sub sandwich, Lucy ate $\frac{2}{6}$ of her sub sandwich, and Evan was really hungry and ate $\frac{3}{4}$ of his sub sandwich! Using the sub sandwiches and number lines above, divide and label each sandwich to show how much Ella, Lucy, and Evan ate.

(Answers on pages 176–177)

EQUIVALENCE AND COMPARISONS OF FRACTIONS

> **NF.A.3** Explain equivalence of fractions in special cases, and compare fractions by reasoning about their size.

1. Which set of fraction models is equivalent?

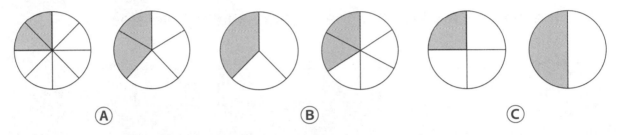

   Ⓐ   Ⓑ   Ⓒ

2. Circle the fractional parts that are equivalent.

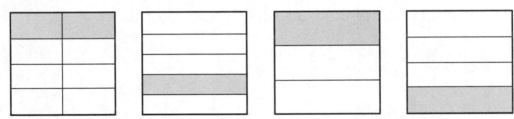

3. Use the grids below and shade $\frac{1}{4}$ of each whole.

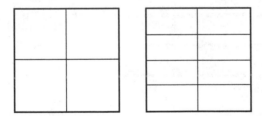

   What do you notice about the shaded regions?

_____

4. How many fourths are equal to 2 wholes?

   Ⓐ $\frac{4}{4}$ Ⓑ $\frac{2}{4}$ Ⓒ $\frac{8}{4}$ Ⓓ $\frac{8}{8}$

   Explain how you found your answer.

_____

Use the fraction wall to answer questions 5–7.

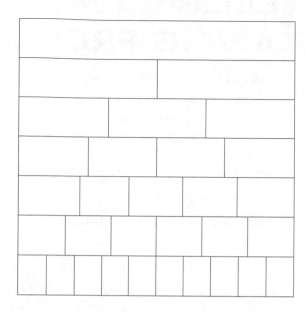

5. Find one fraction that is equivalent to $\frac{1}{2}$. _____

6. Find one fraction that is equivalent to $\frac{2}{3}$. _____

7. Use the fraction wall to explain how you know that $\frac{1}{2}$ is equivalent to $\frac{2}{4}$.

_____

_____

8. Represent the quantity 1 and the quantity $\frac{3}{3}$ on the number line.

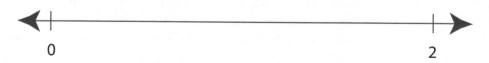

0   2

Compare these two quantities using numbers and words.

_____

_____

(Answers on page 177)

TELLING TIME AND SOLVING PROBLEMS

> **MD.A.1** Tell and write time to the nearest minute and measure time intervals in minutes. Solve word problems involving addition and subtraction of time intervals in minutes, e.g., by representing the problem on a number-line diagram.

1. What time does the clock to the right indicate?

   Ⓐ 2:13

   Ⓑ 3:10

   Ⓒ 2:15

   Ⓓ 1:12

2. Sarah is meeting her friend for lunch at 11:38. Write this time on the clock to the right.

3. Math class begins at 9:15 and ends at 10:15. How long is math class?

   Ⓐ 1 minute   Ⓑ 60 minutes   Ⓒ 60 seconds   Ⓓ 4 hours

4. Describe an activity that would take approximately 5 minutes.

   _____

   _____

5. The family is having a picnic. The park ranger said the picnic must end at 7:45. If a family arrives at 4:00, how long will they have for their picnic? Use a number-line model to solve.

start time   end time

6. The soccer game starts at 2:45 and is 35 minutes long. What time will the soccer game end? Use the clocks below to show the starting and ending time on the clock.

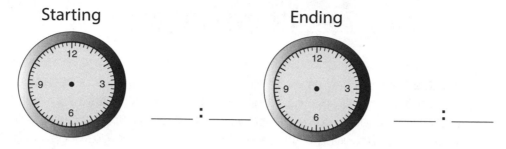

Starting   Ending

_____ : _____   _____ : _____

7. What time will the game be over? Explain your thinking.

_____

_____

8. Jack wants to see a movie. The movie starts at 3:30. The movie is 2 hours and 17 minutes long.

   a. What time will the movie be over? Use a number-line model to explain your reasoning.

     start   end
     time   time

   b. His mother wants him to be home for dinner at 5:55. The theater is 5 minutes from Jack's house. Will Jack be able to do both? Justify your thinking below.

_____

_____

9. An orchestra performed for the children at school. Their performance ended at 3:30. The performance was 1 hour and 12 minutes long. What time did the performance begin? Use a number-line model to represent your thinking.

     start   end
     time   time

(Answers on page 178)

VOLUME AND MASS: MEASURING AND ESTIMATING

MD.A.2 Measure and estimate liquid volumes and masses of objects using standard units of grams (g), kilograms (kg), and liters (l). Add, subtract, multiply, or divide to solve one-step word problems involving masses or volumes that are given in the same units, e.g., by using drawings (such as a beaker with a measurement scale) to represent the problem.

1. Circle the pictures below that would best be measured with grams.

2. Circle the pictures below that would best be measured with kilograms.

Make sure to picture what 1 gram, 1 kilogram, and 1 liter looked like when you measured in your math class.

3. Explain why you made your choices for questions 1 and 2 below.

_____

_____

_____

4. Which item would be measured using liters?
   Ⓐ The amount of punch for a party.
   Ⓑ The height of an elephant.
   Ⓒ The weight of a textbook.
   Ⓓ The amount of grass in a yard.

5. Maggie was buying pop for her birthday party and went to the grocery. She bought four 2-liters of cream pop, three 2-liters of orange pop, and one 2-liter of cherry pop. How many liters of pop does she have for her guests? Show your work with pictures, numbers, and words.

   _____

   _____

   _____

6. The annual pumpkin competition was held in October and people brought in their pumpkins to see whose was the heaviest in the town. David's pumpkin had a mass of 48 kilograms and he won the competition! If Susan's pumpkin had a mass of 39 kilograms, how much smaller than David's pumpkin was hers? Show your work with pictures, numbers, and words.

   _____

   _____

   _____

7. A farmer is loading up apples to take to the farmers' market. Each crate can hold 38 apples. When he weighs the crate he finds out it weighs 8 kilograms. His wagon can hold 6 crates in a load. What is the total mass of those 6 crates in his wagon? Show your work with pictures, numbers, and words.

   _____

   _____

   _____

(Answers on pages 178–179)

PICTURE GRAPHS
AND BAR GRAPHS

MD.B.3 Draw a scaled picture graph and a scaled bar graph to represent a data set with several categories. Solve one- and two-step "how many more" and "how many less" problems using Information presented in scaled bar graphs. *For example, draw a bar graph in which each square in the bar graph might represent 5 pets.*

1. Given the following table listing the cookies at the bake shop, draw a scaled bar graph where each bar represents 10 cookies.

Chocolate chip	160
Sugar	70
Iced	130
Raisin	40

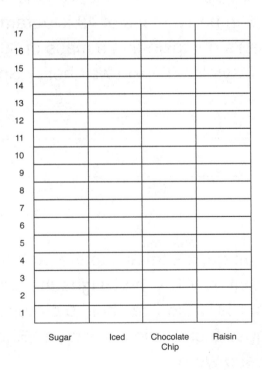

2. Explain what it means to have a scaled picture or bar graph.

_____

_____

Walkers	🚶 🚶 🚶
Bus Riders	🚶 🚶 🚶 🚶 🚶 🚶 🚶
Car Riders	🚶 🚶 🚶 🚶 🚶 🚶 🚶 🚶
Bike Riders	🚶 🚶 🚶 🚶 🚶 🚶

🚶 = 5

3. What does each person represent in the pictograph?

Ⓐ 1

Ⓑ 10

Ⓒ 5

Ⓓ 2

> There is a difference between a picture graph and a pictograph. The pictures used in a picture graph are all representative of one unit. A picture used in a pictograph represents a quantity.

4. Using the graph, how many more car riders are there than bike riders?

_____

5. Verify how you know your answer is reasonable.

_____

_____

For questions 6–7

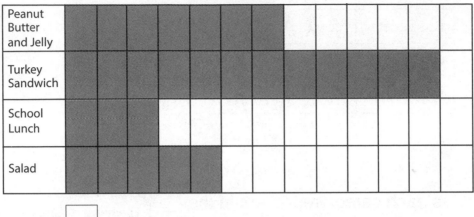

Peanut Butter and Jelly												
Turkey Sandwich												
School Lunch												
Salad												

Scale ☐ Represents 2

6. Using the graph above, how many more students bought a Turkey Sandwich or a School Lunch than Salad or a Peanut Butter and Jelly Sandwich?

Ⓐ 6 Ⓑ 34 Ⓒ 30 Ⓓ 4

7. Justify your thinking when solving the problem above.

_____

_____

For questions 8–10

The students in Mrs. Herraiz's and Mrs. Simonson's class earned
a celebration for positive behavior. Each class took a survey of
how they wanted to celebrate.

Ice Cream Party	20
Game Day	35
Read-In	5
Popcorn Party	15

8. Organize the data collected to create a bar graph below. Be sure
   to include all the parts of a bar graph.

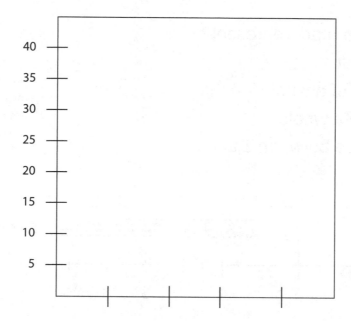

9. How many fewer students wanted a snack for their celebration than
   extra activity during the school day.

   Ⓐ 10   Ⓑ 5   Ⓒ 15   Ⓓ 20

10. Using the data from above, how many students were surveyed?
    Show your thinking below.

_____

_____

(Answers on pages 179–180)

MEASURING LENGTHS AND CREATING LINE PLOTS

MD.B.4 Generate measurement data by measuring lengths using rulers marked with halves and fourths of an inch. Show the data by making a line plot, where the horizontal scale is marked off in appropriate units—whole numbers, halves, or quarters.

1.

1   2

What does the mark represent?

Ⓐ a whole unit

Ⓑ one fourth of a whole

Ⓒ one half of a whole

Ⓓ the distance between 1 and 2

> When using a ruler as a measurement tool, think about how you use a number line. A ruler is a number line.

2.

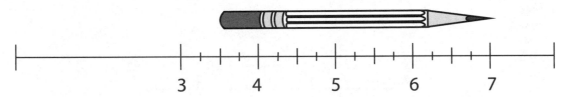

3   4   5   6   7

What is the length of the pencil?

Ⓐ 8 inches

Ⓑ $3\frac{1}{2}$ inches

Ⓒ 5 inches

Ⓓ $7\frac{1}{4}$ inches

3. Blake, Mason, and Manuel wanted to collect data on the length they could kick a soccer ball. They each made a chart to represent the length of three kicks. Using the data that they collected, create a line plot that shows the measurement of their kicks.

Blake's Kicks		Mason's Kicks		Manuel's Kicks	
Kick 1	25 ft	Kick 1	26 ft	Kick 1	$33\frac{1}{2}$ ft
Kick 2	$33\frac{1}{2}$ ft	Kick 2	$25\frac{1}{4}$ ft	Kick 2	$25\frac{1}{4}$ ft
Kick 3	$27\frac{1}{4}$ ft	Kick 3	$33\frac{1}{2}$ ft	Kick 3	25 ft

4. Describe what information you can gather about the data on your line plot.

_____

_____

5.

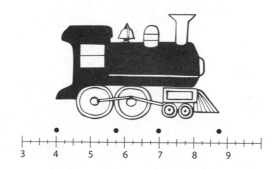

What is the length of the train to the nearest fourth of an inch?

Ⓐ $5\frac{3}{4}$ Ⓑ $4\frac{3}{4}$ Ⓒ $8\frac{3}{4}$ Ⓓ $8\frac{1}{2}$

6. Circle True or False. When measuring an object, you need to start at 0.

True **False**

Justify your reasoning.

_____

_____

7. At Middle Branch Elementary, the student council is making ribbons to give to students as positive-behavior rewards. Below are different ribbons. Measure the ribbons and provide the correct measurements.

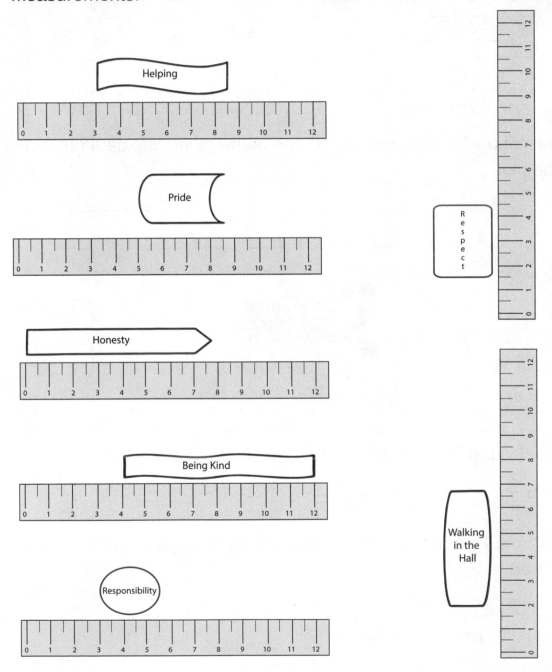

8. Plot the measurements from question 7 on the number line provided.

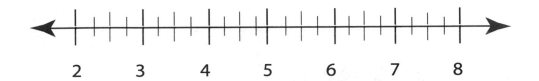

9. If the school wanted to hang all the ribbons that are fewer than $5\frac{1}{4}$ inches, how many ribbons would they collect?

(A) 4

(B) 3

(C) 7

(D) 5

(Answers on pages 180–182)

RECOGNIZING AREA

MD.C.5 Recognize area as an attribute of plane figures, and understand concepts of area measurement.

1. What is area?

_____

_____

2. How do you find the area of a figure?

_____

_____

3. Which attribute describes the area of a shape?

Ⓐ 6 inches

Ⓒ 7 square units

Ⓑ 12 vertices

Ⓓ 6 obtuse angles

4. Using the given shape, describe the shape using all of the attributes you can.

> Attributes are ways of describing; use attributes to describe the sides, shape, color, or size of an object.

_____

_____

_____

5. Matt measured the area of the given shape. He found that the area is 7 square units. Is Matt correct? How do you know?

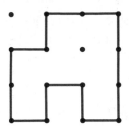

_____

_____

_____

6. Matt measures another shape, and this time he finds that the area is 14 square units. Is Matt correct? How do you know?

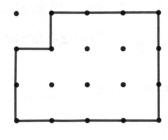

_____

_____

_____

7. What is the area of this shape?

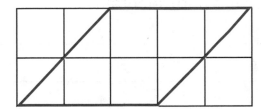

Ⓐ 6 square units

Ⓒ 8 square units

Ⓑ 4 square units and 4 triangular units

Ⓓ $5\frac{1}{2}$ square units

(Answers on page 182)

MEASURING AREA

1. What is the area of the figure?

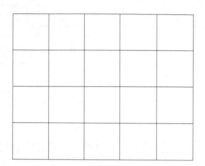

> Remember to measure area
> using square units!

Ⓐ 6 square units   Ⓒ 20 square units

Ⓑ 8 square units   Ⓓ 24 square units

2. What is the area of the figure below? _____ square units

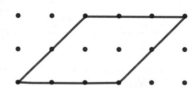

3. Using the shape and your response from question 2, explain how
   you found the area of the parallelogram.

   _____

   _____

4. Draw a shape with an area of 12 square units.

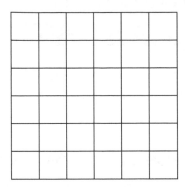

5. Draw a shape with an area of 9 square units.

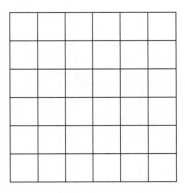

6. Draw a shape below. What is the area of the drawn figure?

_____

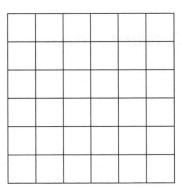

7. Explain how you found the area of your figure in question 6.

_____

_____

(Answers on pages 182–183)

AREA: MODELING, SOLVING, AND RELATIONSHIP

MD.C.7 Relate area to the operations of multiplication and addition.

1. Draw a rectangle with a side length of 5 units and 7 units.

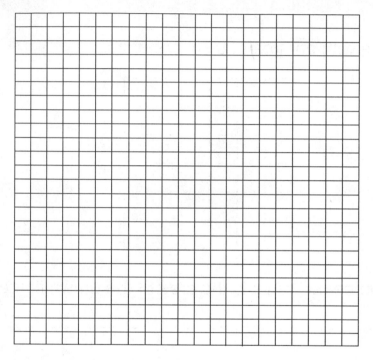

> Multiplication is the same as repeated addition.

2. How can you use multiplication to find the area of a rectangle?

_____

_____

3. If the area of a rectangle is 24 square units, what is a possible length and width of the rectangle?

_____

_____

4. How did you determine the length and width of question 3?

_____

_____

5. The principal at Plain Center Elementary School wants to arrange stepping stones in a rectangle on the playground. The rectangle is 5 blocks long and 6 blocks wide. How many blocks will the principal need?

Ⓐ 30   Ⓑ 20   Ⓒ 36   Ⓓ 25

6.

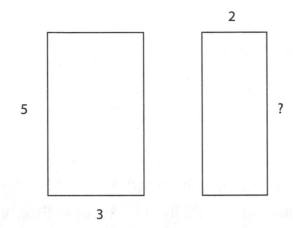

Find the total area of the rectangles above. Show your thinking.

_____

_____

7. Domingo wants to build a vegetable garden. Below is the space he has for the garden. The vegetables he wants to plant must have a certain amount of space. Help Domingo determine the area he has for his vegetable garden, so he can choose the right vegetables.

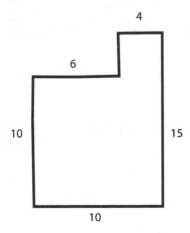

Ⓐ 120 square units   Ⓒ 124 square units
Ⓑ 50 square units   Ⓓ 65 square units

(Answers on page 183)

PERIMETER

MD.D.8 Solve real-world and mathematical problems involving perimeters of polygons, including finding the perimeter given the side lengths, finding an unknown side length, and exhibiting rectangles with the same perimeter and different areas or with the same area and different perimeters.

1. How do you find the perimeter?

   _____

   _____

2. Show a rectangle, with one side length labeled 5 inches. If the perimeter of the rectangle is 26 inches, what is the missing side length?

   (A) 10 inches

   (B) 16 inches

   (C) 5 inches

   (D) 8 inches

3. I have 12 feet of fence to build a dog cage. What are two possibilities I could do to build a cage that has a perimeter of 12 feet?

   _____

   _____

4. Explain how your two cages are different, if they have the same perimeter?

   _____

   _____

   _____

5. The constant area of the classroom reading center is 12 square units. Draw two different representations of the reading center.

6. The perimeter of the square below is 16 feet. What are the side lengths?

> When finding the perimeter, use your knowledge of shape attributes to help you.

Ⓐ 2 feet   Ⓒ 3 feet

Ⓑ 4 feet   Ⓓ 8 feet

7. The one-room schoolhouse is rectangular. It is 18 yards long and 12 yards wide. What is the perimeter of the schoolhouse?

Ⓐ 60 yards   Ⓒ 48 yards

Ⓑ 72 yards   Ⓓ 216 yards

8. The shaded region is the area for the new dog park. What is the perimeter of the dog park?

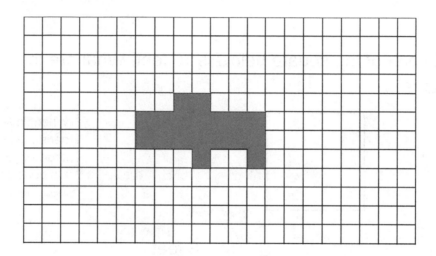

(A) 28 units

(C) 27 units

(B) 24 units

(D) 18 units

9. What is the perimeter of the shape below?

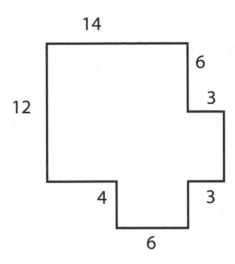

(A) 66 inches   (C) 61 inches

(B) 60 inches   (D) 68 inches

10. Jordan used rubber bands to create a shape on his geoboard. Below is the shape that he created. Jordan said that the perimeter of his shape was 20 units. Jon told Jordan that the perimeter of his shape could not be more than the perimeter of the geoboard. Who do you agree with and why?

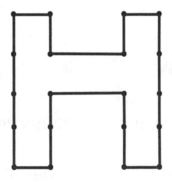

_____

_____

_____

_____

(Answers on page 184)

SHAPE ATTRIBUTES

G.A.1 Understand that shapes in different categories (e.g., rhombuses, rectangles, and others) may share attributes (e.g., having four sides), and that the shared attributes can define a larger category (e.g., quadrilaterals). Recognize rhombuses, rectangles, and squares as examples of quadrilaterals, and draw examples of quadrilaterals that do not belong to any of these subcategories.

1. What attribute do the shapes at the right share?

   Ⓐ All sides are straight and equal

   Ⓑ Four vertices

   Ⓒ All sides are parallel

   Ⓓ Four right angles

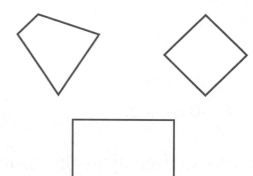

For questions 2 and 3

2. Circle all the shapes above that are categorized as a quadrilateral.

3. Explain why you chose to circle the shapes above.

   _____

   _____

4. Is a rhombus a quadrilateral? Justify your thinking.

   _____

   _____

For questions 5–7

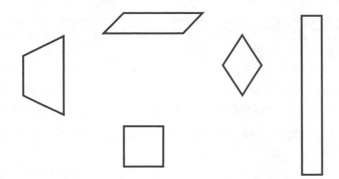

5. How can you describe the shapes above using their attributes?

Ⓐ They have four equal sides.

Ⓑ They have a different amount of vertices.

Ⓒ They are all rectangles.

Ⓓ They are not polygons.

6. Draw a quadrilateral that does not belong with the shapes above.

7. Using the shape you drew above, justify your reasoning why it does not belong, but is still a quadrilateral.

_____

_____

8. What attribute do a rhombus and a rectangle share? Explain your reasoning below.

_____

_____

(Answers on page 185)

PARTITIONING SHAPES TO REPRESENT A FRACTION

G.A.2 Partition shapes into parts with equal areas. Express the area of each part as a unit fraction of the whole. *For example, partition a shape into 4 parts with equal area, and describe the area of each part as $\frac{1}{4}$ of the area of the shape.*

1. Which shape below shows equal area of each part as $\frac{1}{8}$ of the whole shape?

Ⓐ 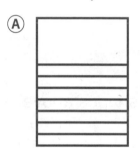 Ⓑ 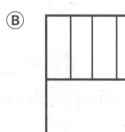 Ⓒ 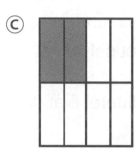 Ⓓ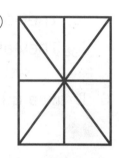

2. Each part of the shape below equally represents _____ of the total figure?

> When partitioning shapes, they must be divided equally in order to show equal area between parts of the whole.

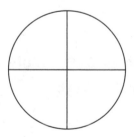

Ⓐ a third   Ⓑ $\frac{1}{2}$ Ⓒ a whole   Ⓓ $\frac{1}{4}$

3. Divide the shape below into 8 parts of equal area.

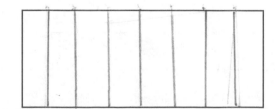

4. How would each equal area part of the rectangle above be represented as a fraction?

Ⓐ $\dfrac{1}{8}$ Ⓑ $\dfrac{1}{2}$ Ⓒ $\dfrac{1}{4}$ Ⓓ $\dfrac{1}{3}$

5. What fraction of the area of the rectangle is not shaded?

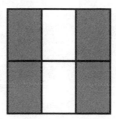

Ⓐ $\dfrac{4}{6}$ Ⓑ $\dfrac{2}{3}$ Ⓒ $\dfrac{2}{6}$ Ⓓ $\dfrac{3}{3}$

6. Circle True or False. Does the square below represent $\dfrac{1}{3}$ equal area parts of the shape?

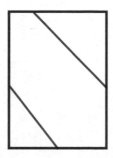

True   **False**

7. Looking at the shape below, how many equal area parts are shaded?

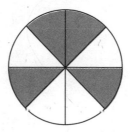

Ⓐ $\dfrac{4}{8}$ Ⓑ $\dfrac{1}{8}$ Ⓒ $\dfrac{3}{8}$ Ⓓ $\dfrac{3}{4}$

(Answers on pages 185–186)

MATH
PRACTICE TEST

My Name: _____

Today's Date: _____

1. Partition the circle and shade in the appropriate parts to represent the fractional part $\frac{6}{8}$.

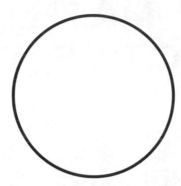

2. When representing a fractional part on a number line, where would you mark 3 equal parts of 3? Choose a letter below.

3. What time does the analog clock show?

   Ⓐ 12:55   Ⓑ 2:55   Ⓒ 1:53   Ⓓ 12:00

4. For which object would you use a kilogram to estimate its mass?
   Ⓐ paperclip   Ⓒ dollar bill
   Ⓑ baseball bat   Ⓓ elephant

5. If each square unit in the shaded area is 1 cm. What number sentence below represents the area of the shaded region?

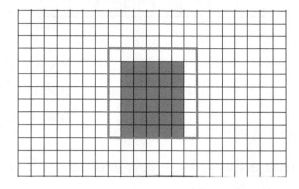

  Ⓐ 7 × 7   Ⓒ 5 + 5 + 5 + 5 + 5

  Ⓑ 6 + 6 + 6 + 6 + 6   Ⓓ 5 × 7

6. Devin's wall has an area of 42 square feet. She has a painting that is 10 feet by 3 feet. Can she hang the painting on her wall? Justify your argument.

_____

_____

_____

7. What is the area of the shaded region?

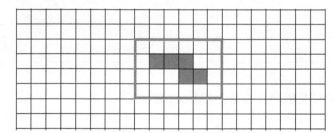

  Ⓐ 5 square units   Ⓒ 6 square units

  Ⓑ 12 square units   Ⓓ 7 square units

8. Which equation matches the multiplication equation 4 × 5?

  Ⓐ 4 + 4 + 4 + 4 + 4   Ⓒ 4 + 4 + 4 + 4

  Ⓑ 5 + 5 + 5 + 5   Ⓓ 6 + 14

9. What is the area of each equal part of the whole shape?

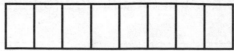

(A) $\frac{1}{8}$ (B) $\frac{1}{2}$ (C) $\frac{1}{4}$ (D) the area cannot be determined without square unit measurements

10. Explain how the two equations below are related. Use pictures and words to explain your thinking.

$$48 \div 8 = 6 \qquad 48 \div 6 = 8$$

_____

_____

11. Samantha earns $7 per hour for babysitting for her next-door neighbor Henry. Henry's parents ask her to babysit this Saturday while they go out to dinner. They ask her to babysit from 6–10 P.M. that night. How much money will Samantha earn for babysitting? Show your work with pictures, numbers, and words.

_____

_____

_____

12. What number makes this equation true?

$$7 \times \underline{\quad} = 21$$

(A) 4   (B) 10   (C) 3   (D) 7

13. If you know $7 \times 6 = 42$, use the commutative property to write another multiplication equation with a product of 42. Explain how this represents the commutative property.

_____

_____

14. Which division equation matches the multiplication equation $5 \times 4 = 20$?

   Ⓐ $20 \div 2 = 10$ Ⓒ $20 \div 5 = 4$

   Ⓑ $4 \div 5 = 20$ Ⓓ $42 \div 2 = 21$

15. Matt is making a video for the school announcements to show the students who received awards this month. The video can only be 60 seconds long. There are 9 students who will each get to have a 5-second clip to say their name and teacher. Will Matt be able to fit all the students into the 60-second video? If so, how much extra time will he have left? Show your work with numbers and words.

_____

_____

_____

_____

_____

_____

16. Complete the input/output chart below and find the rule.

Input	Output
10	20
5	
	14
6	12

Rule: _____

17. Show $\dfrac{3}{4}$ as part of a whole using the rectangle below.

18. Which point on the number line is closer to $\frac{3}{4}$?

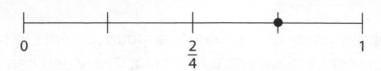

  Ⓐ $\frac{1}{4}$ Ⓑ 1   Ⓒ $\frac{2}{8}$ Ⓓ $\frac{1}{3}$

19. Using the number model to represent fractional parts of a whole, which of the following is true about the parts represented?

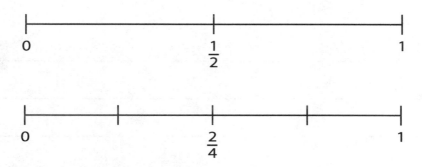

  Ⓐ The two models represent equivalent fractions.

  Ⓑ $\frac{2}{4}$ is larger than $\frac{1}{2}$

  Ⓒ They do not have anything in common.

  Ⓓ They are not partitioned into equal parts.

20. Make the statement below true by using the symbols <, >, =.

$$\frac{6}{6} \quad \boxed{} \quad \frac{3}{3}$$

21. Using the rectangles below, justify your conclusion for question 20.

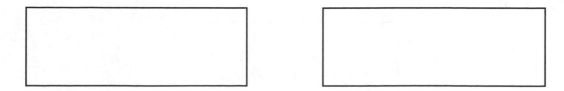

22. Cooper went to soccer practice at 5:33. His mother picked him up from practice at 6:47. How long was Cooper at practice? Show your thinking using the number-line model.

Ⓐ 1 hour and 14 minutes   Ⓒ 1 hour and 4 minutes

Ⓑ 47 minutes   Ⓓ 73 minutes

23. Which unit would you use to estimate the amount of water in your bathtub?

Ⓐ cups   Ⓒ ounces

Ⓑ pounds   Ⓓ gallons

24. If a rectangle is covered by 24 square units, with no spaces, gaps, or overlaps, then what is the area of the rectangle?

Ⓐ 24 square units   Ⓒ 2×12

Ⓑ 12 + 12   Ⓓ The area cannot be determined.

25. When finding the area, what are you counting?

Ⓐ The total space that can be covered by a single unit.

Ⓑ The length of each side.

Ⓒ The amount of single units that are covering a given space.

Ⓓ The area cannot be determined.

26. Draw a picture to represent the equation 8×2. On the lines below, describe your picture and how it accurately represents the equation 8×2.

_____

_____

27. The school's Spirit Club wants to rearrange the cafeteria tables. Before they can do this, they need to determine the area of the cafeteria. Using the diagram below, help the spirit team find the area.

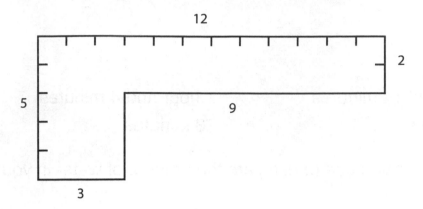

(A) 33 square units

(B) 39 square units

(C) 31 square units

(D) You cannot find the area of this shape since there are multiple lengths.

28. Which division equation matches this picture?

(A) 7 × 4

(B) 28 ÷ 7

(C) 7 ÷ 4

(D) 2 × 10

29. Norah was planting a garden and wanted to plant 6 rows of corn. If she puts 5 corn plants in each row, how many corn plants will she need in all? Show your work with pictures, numbers, and words.

_____

_____

_____

30. What number makes this equation true?

$$45 \div \underline{\hspace{1cm}} = 5$$

Explain how you know.

_____

_____

31. Model using the associative property of multiplication to solve the following equation and explain your work:

$$7 \times 2 \times 5$$

_____

_____

_____

32. What is the missing number to make these equations true? Explain how you know.

$$6 \times \underline{\hspace{0.8cm}} = 36$$

$$36 \div 6 = \underline{\hspace{1.2cm}}$$

_____

_____

_____

33. Lucy went to the Annual Strawberry Festival over the weekend. She took with her $50 she had saved to spend on some delicious treats! She bought a strawberry pie for $17, a jar of strawberry jam for $6, and two containers of chocolate-covered strawberries for $9 each. How much money does Lucy have left over to spend on the rides at the festival? Show your work with pictures, numbers, and words.

_____

_____

_____

_____

34. If you know 6 × 2 = 12, how can you use doubling to help you solve 6 × 4 using the equation 6 × 2 = 12?

_____

_____

_____

35. What does the number of equal parts in a fraction describe?

Ⓐ   How many equal parts are used to make the whole

Ⓑ   The number of the parts shaded

Ⓒ   How to split an object into pieces

Ⓓ   The number of parts that are not shaded

36. What unit fraction is represented on the number line below?

Ⓐ   fourths   Ⓒ   eighths

Ⓑ   halves   Ⓓ   thirds

37. Circle True or False.

The fraction $\frac{4}{1}$ is equivalent to 4.

True   False

38. Austin likes the school breakfasts, so each morning he arrives to school 33 minutes early to eat breakfast. If school starts at 7:50, what time does Austin arrive at school? Use the number line model to show your thinking.

Ⓐ 7:20 A.M.   Ⓑ 7:23 A.M.   Ⓒ 7:17 A.M.   Ⓓ 8:23 A.M.

39. The meat-lovers pizza contains grams of fat from the cheese and meat that is used as the pizza toppings. The mozzarella cheese used has 6 grams of fat on every medium pizza. The meat on the pizza is 8 times the grams of fat than the cheese. How many grams of fat does the medium pizza have?

Ⓐ 48 grams   Ⓑ 54 grams   Ⓒ 14 grams   Ⓓ 64 grams

40. Given the following side lengths of a rectangle, find the area.

9 inches

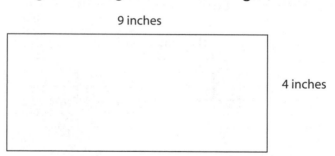

4 inches

Ⓐ 26 square units   Ⓒ 4 + 4 + 4 + 4

Ⓑ 36 square units   Ⓓ 26 inches

41. Which multiplication equation matches the picture below?

Ⓐ 9 × 6   Ⓑ 5 × 6   Ⓒ 6 × 10   Ⓓ 6 × 9

42. Using the unit square provided, show how you can find the area of the given rectangle. Prove your answer.

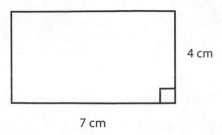

4 cm

7 cm

_____

_____

43. Below is a picture of the space that Clarence has to build a pool in his backyard. When he went to the pool store, the manager asked: What is the area of your space in the backyard? Clarence showed the manager his measurements: 4 + 4 + 4 + 4 + 4 + 4. The manager rewrote the measurements and told Clarence that he could write the measurements a different way. What is another way Clarence can show the area of the space available for the pool?

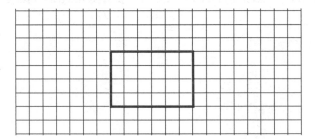

Ⓐ   6 + 6 + 6 + 6 + 6

Ⓑ   24 square units

Ⓒ   4 × 6

Ⓓ   You cannot show the area of the space in another way

44. Write a story problem to match the equation 24 ÷ 4 = 6 using sharing.

_____

_____

_____

_____

45. At soccer practice on Saturday they decide to split the players into teams of 6 to practice passing. There were 54 players at practice on Saturday. How many equal teams of 6 can they make? Show your work with pictures, numbers, and words.

_____

_____

_____

46. Complete the following multiplication and division equations using the given numbers: 4, 32, and 8.

_____ × _____ = _____

_____ ÷ _____ = _____

_____ × _____ = _____

_____ ÷ _____ = _____

47. Grace is practicing her multiplication equations and cannot remember the product of 8 × 6. She knows 8 × 5 = 40. What other fact can Grace use to help her solve 8 × 6? Show your thinking below.

_____

_____

_____

48. Complete the chart below to write a related division and multiplication equation.

Multiplication Equation	Division Equation
$9 \times 3 = 27$	
	$18 \div 3 = 6$

49. Maddox went to the Sweet Shoppe to buy some cookies. He bought 24 chocolate chip cookies and 18 oatmeal cookies. He took the cookies to school the next day to share with his lunch table. If he gives each friend 2 cookies, how many friends can he share his cookies with? Show your thinking with pictures, numbers, and words.

_____

_____

_____

_____

50. How can you use the equation 9×10 to solve 9×9? Show your thinking with equations and words below.

_____

_____

_____

_____

(Answers on pages 186–190)

MATH ANSWERS EXPLAINED

OPERATIONS AND ALGEBRAIC THINKING

Understanding Multiplication (OA.A.1), pages 94–95

1. **B** Each plate or group has 4 cookies on it; therefore, there are 6 groups with 4 in each group. There's often the misconception that the numbers in a multiplication equation do not have to follow a specific order. However, it is important to note that the multiplication symbol in this equation represents *groups of* and the picture has 6 groups of 4 cookies each, not 4 groups of 6 cookies each.

2. **C** The repeated addition equation represents 7 groups of 3. Repeated addition equations represent adding equal groups. This equation is adding 7 equal groups of 3, which can be modeled as the multiplication equation 7×3. There can be a misconception that the numbers in a multiplication equation do not have to follow a specific order. Therefore, you may have thought that the repeated addition equation represents 3×7. However, this equation represents 3 groups of 7, which would be adding 3 equal groups of 7.

3. **A** The skip counting represents counting equal groups by 2. You could then count the number of times that the pattern counts by 2s to determine that there were 7 groups of 2.

4. **$4 \times 5 = 20$**. You could represent the equation 4×5 in multiple formats including 4 circles with 5 in each group, an array with 4 rows with 5 in each row, or a picture depicting 4 groups with 5 in each group. The picture should model 4 groups of 5 instead of 5 groups of 4. You should then find the product of 4×5 using the picture. You could show counting by 5s to find the product of 20, or add the groups of 5 in a repeated addition equation to find the product of 20.

5. **(A) 9 dogs, (B) 36 legs**. Understand that the equation 9×4 means there were 9 groups of 4. Since the story told that Cassidy was counting the legs on dogs, and you know legs come in groups of 4 on a dog, you should interpret that there were 9 dogs. You should then solve the equation 9×4 to find that there were 36 legs in all.

6. Explain that the equation 4×8 represents 4 equal groups of 8. The answer should demonstrate an understanding that the order matters in a multiplication equation, and that this equation should be represented by 4 groups with 8 in each, not 8 groups with 4 in each.

7. No, the equation $3 \times 9 = 27$ is not represented by the repeated addition equation. They do not match because, even though they have the same product of 27, the repeated addition equation shows equal groups of 3. The equation 3×9 means 3 groups of 9. This would be represented by equal groups of 9 being added to make 27, $9 + 9 + 9$. The repeated addition equation in the question is adding 9 equal groups of 3, which would be represented in a multiplication equation as $9 \times 3 = 27$.

Understanding Division (OA.A.2), pages 96–97

1. **4 pieces of candy each**. You should have used the picture of candy and grouped them into 6 groups of 4. You might draw circles around equal groups, or show sharing these pieces of candy among a picture of 6 children. Make sure that the groups have equal amounts in them to model division through sharing.

2. You should draw 4 groups with 7 students in each group to represent the teams of students. Then write the equation: $28 \div 4 = 7$. The equation should match the picture in

which there were 28 students grouped into 4 equal teams; which resulted in groups of 7 students.

3. Describe the two equations as similar because they both start with the same whole of 56 and include the same numbers in the equations. Explain that both equations model division and are related to the multiplication equation $8 \times 7 = 56$. Describe differences in the equations because each equation would be represented differently. $56 \div 8$ could be represented with 56 as a whole shared between 8 equal groups of 7. $56 \div 7$ could be represented as 56 as a whole shared between 7 equal groups of 8.

4. **A and C** Without knowing the context of the division situation, the picture could represent 15 as the whole shared among 3 equal groups, with 5 in each group; or 15 as the whole grouped into equal groups of 5, which creates 3 equal groups.

5. Explain with words that both equations A and C could match the picture, based on your understanding of division as sharing or grouping. The picture could represent 15 as the whole shared among 3 equal groups, with 5 in each group; or 15 as the whole grouped into equal groups of 5, which creates 3 equal groups.

6. **$45 \div 9 = 5$.** Model a strategy for solving $45 \div 9$ that could include repeated subtraction, drawing a picture of grouping 45 into equal groups of 9, drawing a picture of sharing 45 among 9 equal groups, or an array of 45 total in 9 rows. The model should match the equation, but could show grouping or sharing based on the interpretation of the equation. The important thing is that the model is used to determine that the missing part is 5.

7. **Sharing:** Explain that this equation could be represented with sharing by having 27 items in the whole and sharing them among 3 equal groups. This would result in 9 items in each of the groups. You could explain this in a real-world context or by

describing how 27 would be shared in 3 groups with 9 in each group.

Grouping/Partitioning: Explain that this equation could be represented with grouping by having 27 items in the whole and grouping these into equal groups of 3. This would result in having 9 equal groups. You could explain this in a real-world context or by describing how 27 would be partitioned into groups of 3 with 9 groups.

Solving Word Problems (OA.A.3), pages 98–99

1. The cafeteria will have 60 cartons of chocolate milk. Model using equal groups in a picture that represents 5 groups of 12 cartons of milk. Then use a strategy to determine the total cartons of milk. Strategies could include: repeated addition, grouping tens and ones to add using place value, counting cartons of milk using skip counting. Write an equation to model your thinking of 5 groups of 12, $5 \times 12 = 60$. Your words should explain how you solved the problem by explaining that you knew there were 5 equal groups of 12 milk cartons.

2. They will need to paint 40 hopscotch squares for the boards. You could draw a picture depicting 5 hopscotch boards with 8 squares on each board. You could also represent this with a similar picture showing 5 groups of 8. Then use a strategy such as repeated addition, skip counting, or your fluency knowledge of multiplication facts to determine that 5 groups of 8 would create 40 squares. Represent the solution with the equation $5 \times 8 = 40$.

3. There are 12 chocolate pieces in the chocolate bar. Use a picture depicting an array of chocolate pieces with 3 equal rows of 4 in each row. Then use a strategy to determine the total pieces through repeated addition, skip counting, or fact fluency knowledge. You should represent the problem with the equation $3 \times 4 = 12$;

there are 3 equal rows of 4 in each row. Then explain the solution by describing how the array represents the chocolate pieces and how you found the total number of chocolate pieces by explaining your strategy.

4. Beth and Calla will each get 6 pieces of chocolate. You should use the solution from problem 3 to help solve problem 4. If you know there are 12 pieces of chocolate in the chocolate bar, you can then determine that these would be shared with 2 people. Represent this with a picture of 12 items being shared into 2 equal groups. Show an equation modeling sharing, $12 \div 2 = 6$. This shows that 12 items were shared between 2 people, with each of them receiving 6.

5. The baker could arrange the cookies in 8 rows of 3, 3 rows of 8, 4 rows of 6, 6 rows of 4, 2 rows of 12, or 12 rows of 2. This word problem has multiple solutions in which you could create equal rows of cookies. Draw a picture depicting the equal rows of cookies in an array. Any of the above solutions would be correct as long as the picture shows equal rows. Then write an equation to match the array of cookies. Equations should match the number of rows and amount of cookies in each row. For example: 6×4 if the picture and answer show 6 rows of 4 cookies.

6. Each gift bag should have 9 candy hearts inside. Draw a picture to depict sharing 54 candy hearts equally among 6 bags or groups. When you share the candy hearts, you should determine that there would be 9 in each group in order to be equal. Represent the problem with the equation $54 \div 6 = 9$. This equation models that there are 54 items shared into 6 equal groups with 9 in each group.

7. There will be 9 rows of students in the parade. You should model your thinking with a picture of an array with rows of 4. Continue to draw rows of 4 until you have shown the 36 total band members. This picture would then show 9 equal rows of 4 in each row. Write an equation to match the solution. Equations could show a missing factor: ___ $\times 4 = 36$, or could

model division: $36 \div 4 = $ ____. Make sure to accurately write the equation to match the problem. If you were to write 4×9, this would inaccurately match the problem because this equation models 4 rows of 9 in each. You should then explain, using words, the strategy for determining the number of rows.

Determine Unknown Numbers (OA.A.4), pages 100–101

1. **A** Use a multiplication strategy or fact fluency knowledge to determine $4 \times 6 = 24$. Strategies could include: skip counting 4 groups of 6 (6, 12, 18, 24), repeated addition ($6 + 6 + 6 + 6 = 24$), or using the commutative property (if you know $6 \times 4 = 24$ then $4 \times 6 = 24$).

2. **C** Use multiplication or division to help solve this missing-number equation. If you use multiplication, you will determine how many equal groups of 2 are in 18. You could also use division to start with the whole of 18 and divide it into 2 equal parts to determine that there will be 9 in each part.

3. **B** Use your knowledge of multiplication to determine that 5 groups of 6 equal 30. You could also use division to find the missing factor by understanding that 30 shared into equal groups of 6 would make 5 equal groups, so the missing factor would be 5.

4. **4** Your explanation should include the strategy for finding the missing factor. Strategies could include: repeated addition, skip counting, or drawing an array. Use your understanding of the commutative property of multiplication to reverse the factors and determine how many times you need to skip count by 7s to equal 28, or add groups of 7 to equal 28.

5. **6** Explain how you could use division to help solve a missing factor multiplication equation. Explain how the operations of division and multiplication are inverse (opposite) operations. Therefore, you can use division to start with the whole and divide into equal parts with the given factor to find the missing factor.

Explain how if you know the division fact of 48 ÷ 6 = 8, then you could also explain that the given numbers form a fact family that you can use to make multiplication and division equations that are related.

6. **C** You should determine that the missing quotient is 9 by using knowledge of division as sharing or grouping. You could model and solve 45 shared or grouped into 5 equal groups, which would make 9 in each group. You could also use knowledge of multiplication as an inverse operation to division and solve the related multiplication equation of 5 × ___ = 45 to determine that the missing number is 9.

7. **B** Determine the missing dividend is 27 by using knowledge of multiplication and division as inverse operations. When given the divisor and the quotient, use these to multiply and find the dividend. You can also use your understanding of division to model the equation that an unknown whole is divided or shared into 3 equal groups with 9 in each group. After modeling this equation, count the total to find that the missing dividend is 27.

8. **C** Determine the missing divisor is 7 by using knowledge of multiplication and division as inverse operations. When given the dividend and the quotient, use these to set up a missing factor multiplication equation: 6 × ___ = 42, and use multiplication strategies to determine how many would be in each of 6 equal groups to total 42. You could also use division to help find the missing divisor. You know the whole is 42 and it is shared or grouped into an unknown amount of groups. However, you know that each group will have 6; therefore, model this with a picture of equal groups of 6 or repeated subtraction of groups of 6 until you determine the missing divisor.

9. The missing dividend is 32. Explain how you could use multiplication to help solve a missing divisor or dividend division equation. Explain how the operations of multiplication and division are inverse (opposite) operations. Therefore, you can use multiplication strategies to use the given numbers as the factors

in a multiplication equation and find the whole. Explain that if you know the multiplication fact of 8 × 4 = 32, then when dividing the whole of 32 into 4 equal parts, there would be 8 in each part.

10. Complete the multiplication equations: 3 × 7 = 21, 7 × 3 = 21

Complete the division equations: 21 ÷ 7 = 3, 21 ÷ 3 = 7

Properties of Operations for Multiplication and Division (OA.B.5), pages 102–103

1. **A** You should choose answer A as an example of the commutative property of multiplication in which the order of the factors can be reversed and the product stays the same.

2. Use multiplication strategies to model solving the equations 7 × 3 and 3 × 7 to find the product of 21 for both equations. You could use any of the following strategies: drawing an array, a visual model/picture, repeated addition, or skip counting. Your strategies should show how both equations have a product of 21 regardless of the order of the factors.

3. You should model the distributive property in which one of the factors can be distributed, or broken down, and multiplied by the remaining factor to create simpler equations. In this case, you could represent the equation in a variety of ways. These ways could include: solving 8 × 5 and 8 × 1 and then adding these products to get a final product of 48.

4. Distributive Property: C, Associative Property: A, Commutative Property: B

The commutative property is represented with a set of equations in which the order of the factors is reversed with the product remaining the same. The distributive property is represented by a set of equations in which one of the factors can be distributed, or broken down, and multiplied by the remaining factor to create simpler equations. The associative property is represented by a set of equations in which there are more than 2 factors and the equation can be solved by first multiplying any 2 of the factors together to find the product and then multiplying this product by the additional factor to find the final product.

5. Sarah can use the fact 9×2 to help her determine what the product of 9×7 would be because she would then be solving $9 \times (5 + 2)$. Sarah can use her ability to solve 5's facts and solve 9×5 and this would then leave 2 left over when 7 is broken into $5 + 2$. Sarah would then take the two products and add them to find the product of 9×7.

    $9 \times 5 = 45$
    $9 \times 2 = 18$
    so, $45 + 18 = 63$

6. Solve this equation by grouping 2 of the factors together to solve and then multiplying their product by the final factor. The product 4×5 can be solved more easily; then you could use the product 20×2 to find the final product of 40. You could also first solve $5 \times 2 = 10$ and then multiply the product 10×4 for a final product of 40. Either way of solving allows you to solve an easier equation using your $\times 5$ or $\times 10$ facts and then use this strategy to find the final product of 40.

7. **B** These equations represent the distributive property because the original equation of 8×9 has the 8 distributed across the following equations in order to more easily solve 8×9. The 9 is broken into $5 + 4$ and then each addend is multiplied by 8. These 2 products are then added to find the final product of 72.

Division: Unknown Factors (OA.B.6), pages 104–105

1. **1-C, 2-B, 3-D, 4-A** Division and multiplication equations are related as inverse operations and you should be looking for equations that have the same integers. The multiplication equations can aid in solving the division equations.

2. Explain how the multiplication and division equations are related. Demonstrate how a multiplication equation's factors can be used to find the quotient of a division equation. Multiplication and division are inverse operations and therefore the integers in the equations are related. Explain that in division you are taking a whole and sharing or grouping it into equal groups based on the divisor; just as in multiplication you are creating a set number of equal groups based on the factors and finding the total quantity in the groups. You know that 8 equal groups of 6 will equal 48 total in the whole. Then if the whole of 48 is grouped into 8 equal groups there will be 6 in each group.

3. The missing number is 6 to make both equations true. Demonstrate how a multiplication equation's factors could be used to find the quotient of a division equation. You know that 6 equal groups of 5 will equal 30 total in the whole. Then if the whole of 30 is grouped into 5 equal groups there will be 6 in each group.

4. $\mathbf{9 \times 7 = 63}$

5. $\mathbf{7 \times 8 = 56}$

6. $\mathbf{4 \times 5 = 20}$ (these equations could also be written with the factors reversed)

7. $\mathbf{18 \div 6 = 3}$

8. $\mathbf{35 \div 5 = 7}$

9. $\mathbf{24 \div 6 = 4}$ (these equations could also be written with the quotient and divisor reversed)

10. Explain how the multiplication and division equations are related. Demonstrate how a multiplication equation's factors could be used to find the quotient of a division equation. Multiplication and division are inverse operations and therefore the integers in the equations are related. You should explain that in division you are taking a whole and sharing or grouping it into equal groups based on the divisor; just as in multiplication you are creating a set number of equal groups based on the factors and finding the total quantity in the groups.

Solving Two-Step Word Problems (OA.D.8), pages 106–109

1. There are enough chairs for everyone because there are 123 chairs and 123 is more than 120; there will be 3 extra chairs left over.

   You should model with a picture and equations adding the quantities of chairs together: 75 + 48 to determine that there are 123 chairs in all. Then solve the second part of the problem by subtracting 123 − 120 = 3, or by solving a missing addend equation of 120 + _____ = 123 to determine that there are 3 extra chairs. Your picture should show your thinking and should show efficiency, so rather than drawing out all 123 chairs, you could draw a symbol and label the total quantity of chairs. Students in 3rd grade should be able to represent the chairs with a symbol or represent a group of chairs by writing the total number. Your words should explain your strategy of adding the two groups of chairs to find the total, and then comparing this quantity to the needed quantity of 120 chairs to find out if you had enough chairs. Explain that through subtraction or missing addend addition you found that there were 3 extra chairs.

2. Adam spent $24 and John spent $8, so Adam spent $16 more than John.

   Use a picture and equations to model the amount that each boy spent at the book fair. Your picture should show the known quantity that John spent $8 and then should show the equation 3×8 or 8 + 8 + 8 to determine how much Adam spent since he spent 3 times as much as John. The question asks how much more Adam spent than John, meaning you will need to compare the quantities to find out how much greater Adam's quantity is than John's. You could model this with a bar model, picture, or equation to determine that Adam's quantity is $16 greater than John's. Possible equations could include: 8 + _____ = 24, 24 − 8 = _____

3. Nora will have saved $70 for her puppy.

   Your work should model the money Nora saves both from her allowance and the additional $20 from her grandma. You should model multiplication to determine the total savings from her allowance using the equation $10 \times 5 = 50$. Your picture should also represent the additional $20 from her grandma and model adding this amount to the $50 she has saved from her allowance: 20 + 50 = 70.

4. There are 24 pieces of gum shared between 5 people, which will mean they each get 4 pieces with 4 left overs. You should model your thinking with a picture to show the total number of pieces of gum which is found using multiplication: 6 groups of 4 pieces of gum = 24 total pieces of gum; and then the picture should also model sharing the gum between 5 people. When drawing your picture, you will be able to see that the 24 pieces of gum do not share equally among 5 people, which will result in 4 pieces of gum left over. The equations should include multiplication for finding the total pieces of gum: $6 \times 4 = 24$, and division for sharing the pieces of gum: $24 \div 5 = 4$ with 4 pieces left over.

5. The sunflowers will need 56 ounces for the week and the lettuce will need 42 ounces for the week. They will need 98 ounces of water for a week of watering. You should model the 8 ounces of water for the sunflowers and the 6 ounces of water for the lettuce as the groups, and you will need 7 groups of these for the 7 days in a week. You can model this with the equations: $7 \times 8 = 56$ and $7 \times 6 = 42$. When you have found the total water for one week for each plant, combine these amounts to find the total water for one week for both plants. This can be represented with the equation 56 + 42 = 98.

6. Kirk can go to the pool and get a popsicle for 8 days before he runs out of having enough money; after 8 days he will have spent $48 and will have $2 left over. You can approach

the problem in multiple ways. One way to solve it would be to find the total cost of going to the pool and getting a popsicle (4 + 2 = 6) and then dividing the $50 into groups of 6 to find how many days he can go to the pool. You could also use multiplication, and use a guess-and-check method to try a set number of days and increase or decrease based on the product. For example, if you try 5 days, you will find that $5 \times 4 = 20$ (dollars spent entering the pool), and $5 \times 2 = 10$ (dollars spent on popsicles), so 20 + 10 = 30 (meaning he still has $20 left over and can go to the pool more than 5 days). You should model your strategy with a picture to show the cost of both entering the pool and the popsicle over the 8 days he can go before not having enough money.

7. They could order 1 large (8 pieces) and 5 extra large (60 pieces): $1 \times 8 = 8$ and $5 \times 12 = 60$ so, 8 + 60 = 68, 4 large (32 pieces) and 3 extra large (36 pieces): $4 \times 8 = 32$ and $3 \times 12 = 36$ so, 32 + 36 = 68, or 7 large (56 pieces) and 1 extra large (12 pieces): $7 \times 8 = 56$ and $1 \times 12 = 12$ so, 56 + 12 = 68. Use a picture to model the different-sized pizzas and the total amount of slices in order to find a combination that makes 68 pieces exactly. You could set up a table to organize your work to try out each combination of pizzas, or you could use trial and error to try a set number of each pizza and determine the total slices.

8. **C** You should be looking for equations that show rounding, as this is a strategy to help with estimating the answer to an equation. Use your knowledge that rounding to the nearest 100 is found by looking at the digit in the tens place and if it is higher than or equal to 5 groups of 10, then you will round up to the next group of 100, and if it is less than 5 groups of 10, then you will round down to stay at the current group of 100. Therefore, 228 rounds to 200, and 524 rounds to 500; 415 rounds to 400 and 407 rounds to 400.

9. The 2nd graders have brought in 752 pennies and the 3rd graders have brought in 822 pennies. Therefore, the 3rd graders

have brought in 70 more pennies than the 2nd graders.

10. Write estimation equations by rounding each of the distances. 178 when rounded to the nearest 100 would be 200, 103 would round to the nearest 100 and become 100, and 276 would round to the nearest 100 and become 300. Therefore, 200 + 100 + 300 = 600, which is more than their goal of 500 miles. The Colemans traveled a total of 557 miles on their first day. 178 + 103 + 276 = 557

Arithmetic Patterns (OA.D.9), pages 110–111

1. Explain that when you are looking at an addition chart, you could see the sums of 9 by looking diagonally in a line. These equations have a pattern in that as the first integer becomes 1 more, the second integer becomes 1 less. These make the sum of 9 stay constant because as each integer increases by 1 and decreases by 1, this cancels the effects and keeps the sum at 9. You know you have written all the equations if you start with 0 and continue to increase the first integer by 1 until you reach the sum amount, 9. If you were to use any integers more than 9, you would need to write a subtraction equation.

2. This statement is true. When you multiply an integer times 2 you are doubling it. Even numbers are numbers that can evenly be shared into 2 groups or pairs. When you create a double this will always result in being able to then split this product into 2 equal groups.

3. This is true because when you multiply a number by 4 you are creating another double from the $\times$ 2 fact. When you look at the integers 2 and 4, you can double 2 (2 + 2) for a sum of 4. Therefore, when you are solving multiplication equations you can use this doubling knowledge to first solve a doubling equation ($\times$ 2) and then double the product to find the solution to a $\times$ 4 equation. Seven (7) groups of 4 represents adding 7 + 7 + 7 + 7, which can be grouped

into 14 + 14; this equation represents doubling the solution of 7 × 2.

7 × 2 = 14

7 × 4 = 28 = 7 + 7 + 7 + 7

14 + 14 = 28

4.

Input	Output
25	19
14	8
9	3

Complete the above input/output chart by using the rule to subtract 6 from each input number in order to find the output.

Input	Output
16	8
10	5
8	4

Use your knowledge of arithmetic patterns in the above input/output table using the rule of dividing by 2. Then take the input and this number will be divided by 2 in order to find the output or quotient.

Input	Output
6	18
4	12
3	9

Use your knowledge of arithmetic patterns in the above input/output table using the rule of multiplying by 3. Then take the input and this number will be multiplied by 3 in order to find the output or product.

5. The rule is dividing by 4. You have to determine what the pattern is between the input and output integers. You should find that the output integers are smaller; therefore the rule must involve subtraction or division as these are both operations that result in a quantity that is less. Then determine that there is no constant amount that is subtracted, so the rule must involve division.

6.

Input	Output
4	12
1	3
9	27
3	9

Rule: × 3

Find the rule using the two input/output pairs that are given. Using these pairs, determine that the values are increasing; therefore the rule must be addition or multiplication. If you first try addition with the pair 4, 12, you would find that you are adding 8 to the input. If you try this same rule with the pair 3, 9, you will determine that this rule does not work. Use your multiplication strategies of drawing 4 equal groups and finding how many you would need to go in each group to make a total product of 12. Once you determine that 4 × 3 = 12, you should again test this with the pair 3, 9. You will also find that 3 × 3 = 9. You now know that the rule is × 3, which you can use to complete the missing input and output.

7. Explain that 7 × 9 would be one less group of 7. Therefore, when solving you could find that 7 × 10 = 70 and then solve 70 − 7 = 63.

8. Explain that you can use doubling to help you move from a × 2 equation to a × 8 equation.

4 × 8 = 8 + 8 + 8 + 8 = 16 + 16 = 32

8 × 8 = 8 + 8 + 8 + 8 + 8 + 8 + 8 + 8 = 32 + 32 = 64

NUMBERS AND OPERATIONS IN BASE TEN

Rounding Whole Numbers (NBT.A.1), pages 112–113

1. **D** When rounding to the nearest ten, you need to look at the ones place to determine how the number in the tens place will round. In this number, the ones place is a 4, therefore since it is less than 5, the tens place remains the same.

2. **A** When rounding to the nearest hundreds, you need to look at the tens place to determine how the number in the hundreds place will round. In this number the tens place is a 5, meaning 50. Since it is a 5 the hundreds place rounds to the next hundreds value, which would be 900. It is 900 because when moving on the hundreds chart from 800, the next hundreds value is 900.

3a. Any of the following will round to 340

   335, 336, 337, 338, 339, 340, 341, 342, 343, 344

3b. Any of the above numbers will round to 340 when rounded to the nearest ten, because the number in the ones place determines which ten the number is closest to. For example, 338 is closest to 340, as 8 in the ones place indicates that when rounding the number needs to go to the next ten from 30 to 40. The number 342 is closest to 340 as well. The number in the ones place, 2, indicates that when rounding the number remains within the ten.

4. **B** When rounded to the nearest hundred, you must look at the number in the tens place, which in this number is 6 or 60. Since it is a 6 the number in the hundreds place needs to round to the next 100, from 500 to 600.

5. The ✗ should be placed past the midpoint of the line, near the 800. This will indicate an understanding of number relationships when rounding. It is important to see that 780 is 30 from 750 and 20 from 800, which indicates why it is closer to 800 than 750. This problem allows a visual for rounding to the nearest 100.

6. The ✗ should be placed closely near the 350. This will indicate an understanding of number relationships when rounding.

7. The mail carrier would work the Monday Tuesday shift. He would work this shift because there are about 900 pieces of mail that need to be delivered. When rounding the shift, Monday would be rounded to 300 and Tuesday would be 600. Therefore, 300 and 600 is 900. The other shift was about

800 pieces of mail when rounding to the nearest hundred.

8. **Agree.** When rounding a number to the nearest 100, you need to look at the tens place to determine how the number will be rounded. Sam's number is 643, since 40 is less than 50 his number will remain in the 600's. Erin's number is 629, since 20 is less than 50 her number will remain in the 600's. Therefore, Erin is correct in saying that when rounding to the nearest 100, both numbers will round to 600.

Fluently Add and Subtract (NBT.A.2), pages 114–115

1. **796** Use place-value blocks to show how these numbers are composed. Combine like values of hundreds, tens, and ones. You should be able to show this in numbers by 400 + 300 = 700 and 60 + 30 = 90 and 2 + 4 = 6; therefore, 700 + 90 + 6 = 796.

2. Place value was used to combine like values. When using place value, the hundreds were combined to make 700, the tens were combined to make 90, and the ones were combined to make 6. There were 7 groups of hundreds, 9 groups of tens, and 6 single units for ones.

3. When solving this problem, use addition to add up, starting from the smaller number. If you add 100 to 568, you will have 668. You can then add 2 groups of 10 and have 678, 688. You can then add 2 ones to make the next ten which will be 690. If you are having difficulties with this strategy, you may have trouble seeing the relationships between addition and subtraction. You may need more experiences with concrete models and part-part-whole in order to identify how these operations are related.

4. **B** If you subtract the number of people in line for the Speedster from the number of people in line for bumper cars, you will find the difference between the lines. The difference between these two lines will give you how many more people are in line for bumper cars.

5. **998** You should show how you solved the problem. The standard states *fluently* adding numbers to 1000. Therefore, you should be able to complete this quickly by using number relationships and place value.

6. You should be able to explain that you combined like values and used simple number facts to compose larger facts. For example, you know that 7 + 2 is 9, therefore, 700 + 200 is 900. You know that 8 + 1 is 9, therefore 80 + 10 is 90. You know that 2 + 6 is 8. You know that 900 + 90 + 8 is 998. You may also make 782 to 792 from 216. This makes 216 now 206. You may then notice that 6 and 2 is 8 making it 798 and 200, which is 998.

7. If you know that 98 is 2 less than one hundred, then you know that 700 is 2 more than 698. If you are given this problem, and you want to use a visual model or numbers to represent the problem, you must be able to fluently identify number relationships. You should be able to see the problem and identify instantly the relationship that the numbers have, whether that is building a ten or a hundred. If not, practice identifying number relationships between 10s and 100s, along with fact fluency to 10.

8. **A** This number sentence is true, because each side of the equal sign is equivalent to 714. The equal sign means *the same as*. This means that both sides of the equal sign need to equal the same amount.

9. **B** The associative property of addition is when three or more numbers are added together and regardless of the groupings they will equal the same sum.

Multiples of Ten (NBT.A.3), pages 116–117

1. **4 × 10 = 40** Your model should represent 4 groups of 10, represented by rods of 10 place value blocks. You should have drawn 4 rods of 10 to represent the 4 groups of 10. These can then be counted by 10s to find the product of 40.

2. **D** You should determine this solution based on your place value knowledge that 10 × 7 is equal to 7 × 10. The equation 7 × 10 represents 7 groups of 10, which can be solved by counting by 10s for a product of 70. You should also use your understanding of place value to know that 1 × 7 = 7, therefore when you multiply by 10, this product will be 10 times larger in quantity.

3. **B** You should determine this solution based on your place value knowledge of 9 × 10, 9 groups of 10. This equation can be solved by counting by 10s for a product of 90. You should also use your understanding of place value to know that 1 × 9 = 9, therefore when you multiply by 10, this product will be 10 times larger in quantity.

4. You should explain that when you multiply by 10 you are counting groups of 10, therefore the product would be 80 because 8 groups of 10 is 80 (10, 20, 30, 40, 50, 60, 70, 80). You could also explain how you can use your understanding of place value to solve 8 × 1 = 8. Then if you multiply 8 × 10, this solution will be 10 times larger in quantity, which would result in a product of 80.

5. **6 × 40 = 240** You should explain how you found the solution using a picture or words. Explanations could include: a place value drawing showing 6 groups with 40 in each group and a method for grouping and adding these values or using properties of operations to split the equation into 6 × 4 × 10 and then solve these equations by multiplying 6 × 4 = 24, then using your knowledge of place value to multiply 24 × 10 to find the product of 240.

6. You should explain that these equations have the same product because breaking the factor 70 into 7 × 10, in order to solve more easily, can solve the equation 3 × 70. You could explain that in a multiplication equation you can change the order of the factors and have the same product, based on the properties of operations. Therefore, though the factors are different in the equations, their value remains equal and results in an equal product.

7. **D** You can use your knowledge of place value to find the product of 6×9, which is 54, and when you multiply by a multiple of 10 you are making the product 10 times larger. Therefore, you can find the product of 540 for the equation. You could also use your understanding of the properties of operations to solve $6 \times 9 \times 10$ in a similar way. First you would multiply $6 \times 9 = 54$, and then multiply by 10, which makes the value 10 times larger.

8. **A** You can use your knowledge of place value to find the product of 7×7, which is 49, and when you multiply by a multiple of 10 you are making the product 10 times larger. Therefore, you can find the product of 490 for the equation. You could also use your understanding of the properties of operations to solve $7 \times 7 \times 10$ in a similar way. First you would multiply $7 \times 7 = 49$, and then multiply by 10, which makes the value 10 times larger.

9. **$6 \times 10 = 60$** You should show your solution using a picture or words to explain how you solved 6×10. A picture would model 6 groups of 10 fruit snacks in each group, and then you would combine and add these groups or count by 10s to find a product of 60. A written explanation could include representing how to count by 10s, 6 times in order to find a product of 60.

10. **$4 \times 30 = 120$** You should show your solution using a picture or words to explain how you solved 4×30. A picture would model 4 groups of 30 students in each group, and then you would combine and add these groups to find a product of 120. A written explanation could include representing how to add 4 groups of 30.

NUMBERS AND OPERATIONS—FRACTIONS

Building an Understanding of Fractions (NF.A.1), pages 118–119

1a. **4** You should be able to understand that the whole circle pictured is then split into 4 equal parts on the partitioned circle. You should count both the shaded and unshaded parts to determine the parts to make a whole.

1b. **$\frac{1}{4}$** You should understand that the denominator in a fraction represents the equal parts to make a whole. You should understand that the numerator describes the shaded region. Therefore, you should label the shaded part as $\frac{1}{4}$ because there are 4 parts to the whole and 1 of those parts is shaded.

2.

You should divide the square into 4 equal parts. You should then have shaded 1 of the 4 equal parts.

3. You should describe the relationship between the unit fraction, $\frac{1}{4}$, and the fraction $\frac{3}{4}$. You should explain that it takes three $\frac{1}{4}$ pieces to make $\frac{3}{4}$ because $\frac{1}{4} + \frac{1}{4} + \frac{1}{4} = \frac{3}{4}$. You should show an understanding that $\frac{3}{4}$ is related to the fraction $\frac{1}{4}$ because both fractions describe a whole that is divided into 4 equal parts.

4. You should divide the rectangle into 8 equal parts and shade 6 of those parts. You should demonstrate an understanding that $\frac{6}{8}$ can be represented by shading six $\frac{1}{8}$ pieces. You should explain that the numerator is important in knowing the parts of the whole to be shaded. In the fraction $\frac{6}{8}$, the numerator, 6, tells you that 6 of the $\frac{1}{8}$ sections need to be shaded.

5. The 3 represents the denominator in this fraction. The denominator tells how many equal parts it takes to make the whole. In this fraction, the whole is partitioned into 3 equal parts.

6. The 6 represents the denominator in this fraction. The denominator tells how many equal parts it takes to make the whole. In this fraction, the whole is partitioned into 6 equal parts.

7. Divide the triangle into two halves by drawing a line down the middle. Shade in one of the halves.

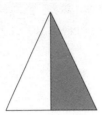

Fractions on a Number Line (NF.A.2), pages 120–121

1.

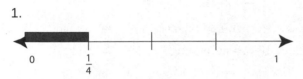

You should demonstrate an understanding that the fraction $\frac{1}{4}$ can be made on a number line by partitioning the number line into 4 equal parts.

2. Your answer should reflect your understanding that you need to divide the number line into 4 equal parts because the denominator in a fraction tells the number of parts to make the whole. You can break it into 2 equal parts and then divide it again to make 4 equal parts. You should also explain that you could label the fraction $\frac{1}{4}$ on the number line by shading 1 out of 4 equal parts or marking the line that shows the end of 1 of the 4 equal parts.

3. **A** Divide the number line to show each of the fractions on the number line and determine which is closest to $\frac{1}{2}$. You could also use your understanding of fractions and equal parts to determine that a line divided into 3 equal parts will have larger parts than a line in 4 or 10 equal parts. You should not choose choice D because this refers to the whole. The whole is larger than $\frac{1}{2}$ and is

represented by the number 1 on the number line.

4.

You should divide the number line into 8 equal parts. You can do this by using your knowledge of equality and number sense to first divide the line into 2 equal parts, and then split these parts to form 4 equal parts, and again split the parts to form 8 equal parts. You should then label the fractions based on the number of parts represented on the number line.

5. You should explain that the fraction $\frac{5}{8}$ is represented on the number line by labeling the point where 5 of the 8 equal pieces end.

6.

You should first understand that the vocabulary word iterate means to repeat the same unit. You should have repeated the unit $\frac{1}{3}$ to divide and label $\frac{2}{3}$ and $\frac{3}{3}$ on the number line. Their parts should be equal in size to demonstrate an understanding of equality in fractions. You should also label $\frac{3}{3}$ and not use the label 1; though they have the same value, the question refers to iterating units.

7.

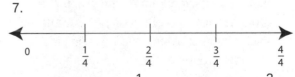

Repeat the unit $\frac{1}{4}$ to divide and label $\frac{2}{4}$, $\frac{3}{4}$, and $\frac{4}{4}$ on the number line. Their parts should be equal in size to demonstrate an understanding of equality in fractions. You should also label $\frac{4}{4}$ and not use the label 1; though they have the same value, the question refers to iterating units.

8. **D** You should use your knowledge of number lines and fractional parts to answer this

question. You should understand that $\frac{5}{6}$ is $\frac{1}{6}$ away from a whole or 5 equal parts on a number line divided into 6ths. This would make the fraction $\frac{5}{6}$ closest to 1 whole rather than $\frac{1}{2}$.

9. Ella's sub should be divided into 8 equal parts and the fraction $\frac{3}{8}$ should be shaded or labeled to show how much Ella ate.

Lucy's sub should be divided into 6 equal parts and the fraction $\frac{2}{6}$ should be shaded or labeled to show how much Lucy ate.

Evan's sub should be divided into 4 equal parts and the fraction $\frac{3}{4}$ should be shaded or labeled to show how much Evan ate.

Equivalence and Comparisons of Fractions (NF.A.3), pages 122–123

1. **B** Look at the circles and their fractional parts to find the set of circles with equal fractional parts. You should see that though the total parts to make the whole differ, the shaded amount remains constant in answer B with $\frac{1}{3}$ and $\frac{2}{6}$.

2. You should circle the fraction $\frac{2}{8}$ and $\frac{1}{4}$. These fractional parts are equivalent because the fraction $\frac{2}{8}$ has the same relationship to the whole as the fraction $\frac{1}{4}$.

3. You should shade 1 out of 4 parts on the first grid and 2 out of 8 parts on the second grid.

What do you notice about the shaded regions?

The shaded regions are equal in amount in both grids though the fractional pieces to make the whole vary.

4. **C** You should use your knowledge of the relationships between fractional pieces and the whole and how they are equivalent. You know that $\frac{4}{4}$ is equal to 1 whole, therefore 2 wholes would be equal to $\frac{8}{4}$. You could

draw a visual model to represent your thinking and model how 2 wholes can be cut into fourths, creating 8 fourths total. You could also use your knowledge of numbers and operations to prove that if there are 4 fourths in 1 whole, you would double this for 2 wholes; therefore 4 + 4 = 8 fourths.

5. Fractions equivalent to $\frac{1}{2}$:

$$\frac{2}{4} \quad \frac{4}{8} \quad \frac{3}{6} \quad \frac{5}{10}$$

You should use the visual model of the fraction wall to find the piece equal to $\frac{1}{2}$ and then use this fractional piece as a guide to find other fractional amounts that equal its size.

6. Fraction equivalent to $\frac{2}{3}$: $\frac{4}{6}$

You should use the visual model of the fraction wall to find the pieces equal to $\frac{2}{3}$ and then use these fractional pieces as a guide to find other fractional amounts that equal its size.

7. You could shade in each set of fractional pieces to represent $\frac{1}{2}$ and $\frac{2}{4}$ to see their equivalence based on the visual representations matching in size. The two parts are represented using the same size whole in the fraction wall, allowing you to make the comparison visually.

8. You should label the quantity 1 at the midpoint on the number line based on your knowledge of number relationships, that 1 is equidistant from 0 and 2. You should also label $\frac{3}{3}$ on the number line at the midpoint. You should determine where this quantity exists by using your understanding of fractional pieces and their equivalence to the whole. Therefore, $\frac{3}{3}$ is equal to 1. When comparing these quantities, you should use the symbol = to demonstrate your understanding of how whole numbers relate to fractional pieces. Your words should explain how you know that 3 thirds is the same amount as 1 whole.

MEASUREMENT AND DATA

Telling Time and Solving Problems (MD.A.1), pages 124–125

1. **A** You should pick choice A because the hour hand is on the 2 and the minute hand is 3 minutes past 10. Therefore it is located at 13 minutes. This indicates that the time is 2:13.

2. You should accurately draw a shorter hand on the number 11 and a longer hand 3 "minute" marks past the 7, towards the 8. The 7 is the same at 35 minutes and the 8 is the same as 40 minutes. If the longer hand is drawn 3 minutes past the 7, then it is at 38 minutes. When showing the time on the clock, it is important that there is a long and short hand.

3. **B** You should be able to understand the length of time at various intervals. You should know that 60 minutes is the same as 1 hour. Curricular areas are typically at least 60 minutes in length.

4. You can describe any activity that can be accomplished reasonably within 5 minutes. Examples of these activities may include brushing teeth, putting on shoes, getting dressed, walking down the hallway, packing a lunch, and so on.

5. **3 hours and 45 minutes.** Begin at 4:00 and count forward adding hours until 7:45. Or you can start at 7:45 and count backwards until 4:00.

6. You should write 2:45 on the starting clock. This clock will have a short hand on the 2 and the longer hand on the 9. The longer hand is located on the 9 because when counting by 5's the 9 is equivalent to 45 minutes on a clock. You can also use multiplying or dividing. For example, 9 × 5 is 45 or 45 divided by 5 to know that the minute hand is on the 9. The ending clock will be 3:20. The short hand is on the 3 and the longer minute hand is on the 4.

7. **The game will be over at 3:20.** You can count by 5's 35 minutes and explain this by saying "I counted from 45, 50, 55, 60, 05,

10, 15, and 20." Or you may use your knowledge of quarter hours to identify that 45 to 15 on a clock is 30 minutes and 5 more minutes from 15 is 20. This equals 35 minutes. Another strategy may be to count by 10's, from 45–55 is 10, 55–05 is 10, 05–15 is 10 and 5 more is 35 minutes.

8a. You should begin your number line at 3:30 and make 2 larger hops that represent the hours, from 3:30 to 4:30 to 5:30. You can then break down 17 to 10 and 7 minutes to add efficiently and accurately. You can represent this by making a smaller hop from 5:30 to 5:40. Next you should add the remaining 7 minutes with a smaller hop from 5:40 to 5:47.

8b. **Yes, he will be able to do both.** This is because the movie will end at 5:47. If his mom wants to have dinner at 5:55 he will be home in time for dinner. Since the theater is 5 minutes from his house, he will be home at 5:52. This time is before 5:55.

9. **2:18** You should start on the left side and label the number line model 3:30. You should then hop towards the left 1 hop to represent 1 hour and label this 2:30. Then you should break up the 12 minutes to 10 and 2. You should then make a hop by 10 minutes from 2:30 to 2:20 and label it 10 minutes. You should then hop the remaining 2 minutes from 2:20 to 2:18. Since you are using the number line model to represent time, your understanding of number relationships is critical.

Volume and Mass: Measuring and Estimating (MD.A.2), pages 126–127

1. You should have circled the paperclip and pencil.

2. You should have circled the pineapple, dog, and textbook. You should have an understanding of estimating mass using grams and kilograms. A student could use their benchmark that 1 kilogram is about 1 textbook. Therefore, you would be looking for objects that are heavier in mass to measure with kilograms.

3. You should explain how you used a bench-mark of 1 gram and 1 kilogram to help you decide which measurement unit was most appropriate. You could explain that 1 gram is similar in mass to 1 paperclip; therefore, grams are used to measure lighter objects. It would take a large number of grams to measure a heavy object like a cat and it would be more efficient to use a kilogram unit. You could also explain that 1 kilogram is similar in mass to 1 textbook; therefore, kilograms are used to measure heavier items in comparison to grams.

4. **A** You should use your understanding that liters is a measure of volume and is used to measure liquid items. Therefore, you would select choice A.

5. **Maggie has 16 liters of pop for her guests.** You should model this problem with a picture showing the different kinds of pop in 2-liter containers. You can then solve this problem with an equation to add up the groups of 2. Though there are three different kinds of pop, they all are sold in amounts of 2-liters. You could use a multiplication equation: $8 \times 2 = 16$ to show your thinking or use repeated addition to add up the 8 groups of 2 from your picture to find that there are 16 total liters of pop.

6. Susan's pumpkin was 9 kilograms smaller than David's pumpkin. You should model your thinking with a picture to show the two pumpkins with their mass labeled. You should then solve the problem using subtraction or missing addend addition: $48 - 39 = $ _____ or $39 + $ _____ $= 48$.

7. **The crates' mass is 48 kilograms in all.** You should show your work with a picture of 6 crates that are each 8 kilograms. Your picture could then model adding these groups of 8 in order to determine the total kilograms. You could use numbers to represent your thinking through multiplication, $6 \times 8 = 48$, or repeated addition, $8 + 8 + 8 + 8 + 8 + 8 = 48$.

Picture Graphs and Bar Graphs (MD.B.3), pages 128–131

1. The graph should have 16 for chocolate chips, 7 for sugar, 13 for iced, and 4 for raisin. This is because each bar or square is representing 10.

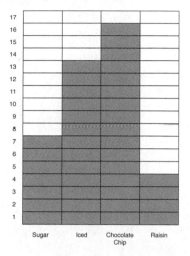

2. A scaled picture or bar graph means that each bar or picture represents a quantity. For every picture on the graph it equals a number more than 1. The scaled picture is given near the graph.

3. **C** Each person in the pictograph represents 5 people. The scale is 5 to one person. This is shown near the pictograph. The scale can change on each pictograph.

4. **15** There are 15 more car riders than bike riders.

   (The explanation is the answer to number 5.)

5. To verify that the answer is reasonable, you need to explain why your answer to number 4 makes sense mathematically. You can do this by writing how you solved the problem. You need to be able to identify that although there are 9 car riders, each picture is equivalent to 5 people. Therefore there are 45 car riders and 30 bike riders. Subtract 30 from 45 to get 15.

6. **A** (Explanation is in number 7.)

7. There were 6 more students who bought turkey or a school lunch. You get this number by adding turkey and school lunch together.

You then add salad and peanut butter and jelly together. The total of the turkey and school lunch is 30 (24 and 6 which equals 30). The total of salad and peanut butter and jelly is 24 (10 and 14 is 24). The difference between 30 and 24 is 6. Therefore, there were 6 more students who bought turkey or school lunch than salad or peanut butter and jelly.

8. The bar graph should include a title, a scale, a scale label, categories, and accurately reflect the data in the table.

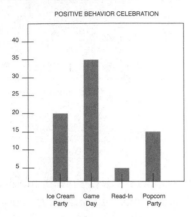

9. **B** When solving for this problem, you need to be able to sort the data into categories as snacks and activities. Once the data is sorted, you can then determine how many students wanted snacks (popcorn and ice cream; 15 + 20 = 35) and how many students wanted an extra activity (read-in and game day; 5 + 35 = 40). After finding the total for each, you would then need to find the difference between 35 and 40 in order to appropriately answer how many fewer students wanted snacks than a celebration.

10. **20 + 35 + 5 + 15 = 75 students were surveyed.** To find the total number of students surveyed, you need to add all of the numbers together.

Measuring Lengths and Creating Line Plots (MD.B.4), pages 132–135

1. **C** The mark is in between 1 and 2. The mark represents half of the distance between 1 and 2. The distance from 1 to the mark and 2 to the mark are the same. Therefore, it is half of a whole. It is not choice B, because the mark would signify $\frac{2}{4}$ of the whole, not $\frac{1}{4}$.

2. **B** The pencil is $3\frac{1}{2}$ inches long. You can show this by moving from $3\frac{1}{2}$ to $4\frac{1}{2}$ is 1 inch, from $4\frac{1}{2}$ to $5\frac{1}{2}$ is 1 inch, from $5\frac{1}{2}$ to $6\frac{1}{2}$ is 1 inch, and from $6\frac{1}{2}$ to 7 is half of an inch. Therefore, the distance is $3\frac{1}{2}$ inches long.

3. You should be able to mark each measurement at the appropriate place including the halves and fourths. Above each measurement you should place an ✗ to indicate that was 1 kick. There should be 2 ✗'s above the number 25 and $25\frac{1}{4}$. There should be 1 ✗ above the numbers 26 and $27\frac{1}{4}$.

There should be 3 ✗'s above the number $33\frac{1}{2}$. Although the half and fourths are not marked with numerals, you should be able to identify what the measurement is based on your understanding of fractional parts to make a whole.

4. You should be able to look at the line plot and indicate that all three boys were able to kick the ball $33\frac{1}{2}$ feet. Two boys were able to kick the ball 25 and $25\frac{1}{4}$ feet. There was only one kick to 26 and $27\frac{1}{4}$ feet. The boys had a total of nine kicks. It is important that you are able to identify what the line plot is showing and the information that can be gained.

5. **B** The train is $4\frac{3}{4}$ inches long. When you are finding the measurement of the train it is the distance the train is from the beginning to the end mark. The ruler does not begin at 0. Therefore, you need to understand that a measurement is a distance of an object not a starting and ending number. From 4 to 5 is 1 unit, 5 to 6 is 1 unit, 6 to 7 is 1 unit, and 7 to 8 is 1 unit, which is a total of 4 whole units. The train ends on three of four marks within the unit, which is $\frac{3}{4}$. Therefore the total distance of the train is $4\frac{3}{4}$ inches.

6. **False.** When measuring an object it is not about what number you begin and end with. It is the distance between the number where you started and the number where you end. Therefore, whether you begin at 3 and end at 6 or begin at 4 and end at 7, your measurement length is still 3 units.

7.

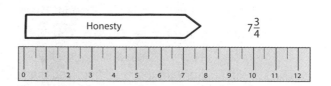

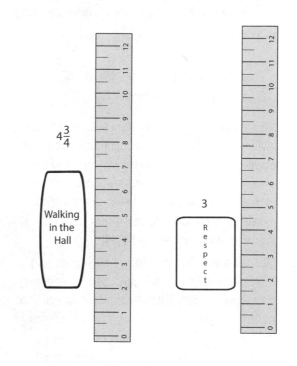

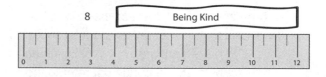

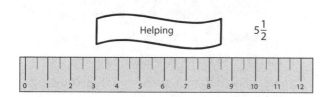

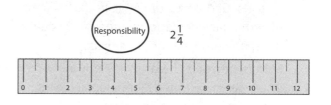

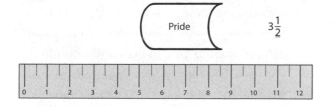

8.

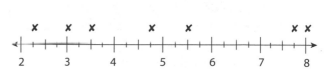

9. **A** The school would collect 4 ribbons. There are 4 ribbons that are less than $5\frac{1}{4}$ inches. The others are more than this length. If you have difficulties with this question, you may not understand what fewer means. Additionally, you may need support in understanding the difference among $\frac{1}{4}$, $\frac{1}{2}$, and $\frac{3}{4}$.

Recognizing Area (MD.C.5), pages 136–137

1. You should understand that area is an attribute of a shape, just as you can describe a shape with its sides, vertices, and angles, you can also describe its area. You should also explain that area measures the space inside of a shape and is measured with square units that are iterated.

2. Describe how area is found by measuring the space inside of a figure and by counting the square units. These square units cannot have any gaps or overlaps when covering the inside of the shape. You could also explain that multiplication or addition can be used to help determine the area of a shape when the side lengths are given.

3. **C** Area measures the space inside of a figure and is found by counting the total square units. The other attributes are ways that you can describe a shape but do not refer to the area of the shape.

4. The rectangle has 4 sides, 4 right angles, 4 vertices, and 2 sets of parallel sides, 4 sets of perpendicular sides, an area of 12 square units, and a perimeter of 14 units.

5. **Matt is correct; the area is 7 square units.** Describe your strategy for determining the area by counting the square units that are inside of the given outlined shape. You could have modeled drawing the squares inside of the shape using the given dots. You could also explain how you could have used addition to find the total area if you grouped the square units within the shape.

6. **Matt is not correct; the area is 11 square units.** Describe your strategy for determining the area by counting the square units that are inside of the given outlined shape. You

could have modeled drawing the squares inside of the shape using the given dots. You could also explain how they could have used addition to find the total area if you grouped the square units within the shape.

7. **A** Use the given trapezoid and count the total square units inside of the shape. You will need to use your knowledge that area is measured in square units, not triangular units as in choice B. You will then have to count the complete square units as well as the $\frac{1}{2}$ squares to make additional whole square units. You should count 4 whole square units and $4\frac{1}{2}$ square units, which would combine to make 2 whole square units. This would then equal a total area of 6 square units.

Measuring Area (MD.C.6), pages 138–139

1. **C** The area is 20 square units. You should have used your understanding of area as the measure of square units inside of a figure. You could have counted the square units and used repeated addition or multiplication to find the total square units of the rectangle.

2. **The area is 6 square units.** You would have had to use your understanding of area as the measure of square units inside of a figure. You could have counted the square units but would also have to combine the $\frac{1}{2}$ square units to make whole square units inside of the trapezoid. There are 4 whole square units and $4\frac{1}{2}$ square units, which would combine to make a total of 6 square units.

3. You should demonstrate an understanding of looking both at whole square units and partial $\frac{1}{2}$ square units. You should explain how you combined the $\frac{1}{2}$ square units to form whole square units when counting and determining the area of the parallelogram.

4. You should be able to use your understanding of area and polygons to draw a figure with a given area. This shape could include

whole and partial square units within it as long as the total square units are 12.

5. You should be able to use your understanding of area and polygons to draw a figure with a given area. This shape could include whole and partial square units within it as long as the total square units are 9.

6. You should draw any shape on the given geoboard. The shape should be a closed figure in order to determine the area, which is found by measuring the space within the figure. You should then find the area of your figure by counting the square units within the shape. If your shape includes partial square units, you will have to combine and count these as well to determine the total area.

7. Your explanation should show that you are able to find the area by counting the square units, using repeated addition or multiplication to find the total square units. This explanation could also include equations to model your thinking. You could also explain how you combined partial square units to form whole square units when finding the total area of your figure.

Area: Modeling, Solving, and Relationship (MD.C.7), pages 140–141

1. You should draw a rectangle. The shape should have 2 opposite sides that are 5 units long and 2 opposite sides that are 7 units long. You can draw a rectangle horizontally or vertically.

2. Multiplication can be used to find the area of a rectangle by multiplying one of the side lengths by the opposite side length. Multiplication is repeated addition, so if one side length is 3 and the other side length is 2, you can find the area by adding 3 + 3 or 2 + 2 + 2. This is also represented by 2×3 (2 groups of 3) or 3×2 (3 groups of 2). Area is the total amount of space covered.

3. Your response may be one of the following; 12 and 2, 3 and 8, or 4 and 6. Think about how 24 can be composed through addition

or multiplication by using two numbers. It may help to draw a rectangle and show how you can create an area of 24 and count the two side lengths.

4. You should describe how you solved question 3 in detail. For example, explain how you know that 8 and 3 make 24. Therefore, if the shape had a side length of 8 and repeated the length 3 times, the area is 24 square units. You could also describe the process by explaining that you drew 6 lines making columns (across, horizontally) and then drew 4 lines making rows (up and down, vertically). You then added 6 + 6 getting 12, with 6 more being 18 and 6 more being 24.

5. **A** The principal will need 30 blocks. This can be determined by multiplying 5×6 or 6×5. You may also find the answer by adding 5 + 5 + 5 + 5 + 5 + 5 or 6 + 6 + 6 + 6. You could draw a picture and count each square unit 1 at a time, but you would be better off building an efficient strategy of addition or multiplication to solve area problems.

6. **The total area is 25 square units.** The area of rectangle 1 is 15 square units. This is because 5×3 is 15. The other rectangle side lengths are 2 and 5. This is known because the two rectangles when next to each other have identical lengths. Although the one length is not given it can be assumed that if the opposite rectangle is the same length, then the missing side length would be 5.

7. **A** The answer is A because when you find the area of the two rectangles within that shape one area is 100 and the other is 20. This is found by multiplying 10×10, which equals 100. The other rectangle side lengths are 5 and 4. The side length 5 is found because the total length of the longest side is 15, and the larger square uses 10 square units of the 15. Therefore, there are 5 square units left, which is the side length of the missing side. If choice B is chosen, you may have found the perimeter instead of the area.

Perimeter (MD.D.8), pages 142–145

1. The perimeter is found by adding all the side lengths together, to find the total distance around a space. The perimeter is not the amount of space covered, but the distance around a given region.

2. **D** The missing side length is 8 inches. The opposite sides of a rectangle are equivalent (have the same length). Therefore, if 5 inches for 1 side was given, then you know that the distance of the opposite side is 5, so the total distance of the 2 sides equals 10 inches. If the perimeter is 26 inches, and you subtract the known 10 inches, there are 16 remaining inches left between the 2 sides. If the 2 sides have to be the same distance because it is a rectangle, you get 8 + 8 equals 16. Therefore, the missing side length is 8 inches.

3. The dog cage lengths can vary. It is important that the shapes are closed figures. You need to demonstrate an understanding that the perimeter equals the side lengths added together. You are not multiplying the side lengths, as this is how area is found. Some examples of possibilities include a square that has a side length of 6, or a rectangle that has side lengths of 8 and 4. You could also draw a polygon that has all different side lengths. When determining if your idea makes sense, you need to make sure when all sides are combined, they equal 24.

4. The two cages have the same perimeter because all the sides when added together equal 12 feet. They are different because the lengths of each side are different, causing the dog's cage to be a different shape or have a different distance among the side lengths. You could also find the area to show they are different.

5. You should draw 2 shapes that have the same area, but different perimeters. The representation could be a rectangle with side lengths of 3 units and 4 units, because $3 \times 4 = 12$. The representation could also be a rectangle with side lengths of 6 units and 2 units, because $6 \times 2 = 12$. The area is the same, but the perimeter is different.

6. **B** If the perimeter total is 16 feet, each side length is 4 feet. A square has 4 equal sides. Therefore, each side is the same length. 4×4 is 16 or $4 + 4 + 4 + 4 = 16$. If you know that half of 16 is 8 and half of 8 is 4, then you know if a square has a side length of 4 feet, the total perimeter will be 16 feet.

7. **A** The perimeter of the schoolhouse is 60 yards. This is found by adding up all of the side lengths. Since it is a rectangle, you know that two sides are 18 yards and two sides are 12 yards. Therefore, $18 + 18 + 12 + 12$ is 60 yards. If you use only one of the lengths, you may need to think about the attributes of shapes and their relationship to perimeter. If your choice was D, you found the area, not the perimeter.

8. **B** The perimeter of the shaded region is 24 units. This can be found by adding all of the sides around the shaded region. It is important that a side is used only one time. You are not counting the number of shaded squares, as that is the area.

9. **A** The perimeter of the shape is 66 inches. When finding the perimeter of the shape, you need to determine the missing lengths. They can be found by finding how the missing lengths are related to those that are already given. One of the missing lengths is 8 inches. This is found by identifying that the opposite side is 14 inches, and the bottom part of the figure, shows the opposite side is 6 inches. Therefore, the remaining portion of the side is 8 inches ($14 - 6 = 8$). The other side can be found by noticing the opposite side length is 12 inches. On the opposite side of 12, one of the lengths is given as 6. Therefore, if you know half of 12 is 6 or $6 + \_\_\_\_ = 12$, you can identify the other missing side length is 6.

10. Jordan is correct. The perimeter of his object is 20 units. The perimeter of the geoboard is 18 units. Jordan's design has a greater perimeter distance than the geoboard because his design also uses the inside parts to create new lengths, and this causes the perimeter to have additional sides.

GEOMETRY

Shape Attributes (G.A.1), pages 146–147

1. **B** All of the shapes are quadrilaterals, allowing any shape that has 4 angles, 4 sides, or 4 vertices to have similar attributes. The answer is B because all the shapes above have 4 vertices (this is plural for vertex). A, C, D do not apply because not every shape has these attributes.

2. You should circle the square, rhombus, rectangle, and trapezoid. These shapes should be circled.

3. You should be able to identify what a quadrilateral is, thus justifying your reasoning for circling the shapes. For example, the shapes circled are quadrilaterals because they are all closed shapes, and they all have 4 sides, 4 angles, and 4 vertices. When shapes have a shared attribute, they can be categorized with other shapes.

4. Yes. A rhombus is a quadrilateral because a quadrilateral is a closed shape and has 4 sides and angles. A rhombus has 4 sides, 4 angles, and is closed. Therefore, a rhombus can be categorized as a quadrilateral.

5. **C** A square is a rectangle but a rectangle is not a square. The shared attributes of a rectangle and square are 4 right angles, 4 straight sides, 4 vertices, 2 sets of parallel lines, and a closed shape. However, a square also has 4 sides of equal length where a rectangle does not. Additionally, all the shapes are polygons.

6. You can draw a rhombus, trapezoid, or an irregular quadrilateral. The reason that any of these shapes do not belong is because the shapes are all squares or rectangles. Therefore, a rhombus, trapezoid, or irregular quadrilateral does not have 4 right angles or 2 sets of parallel sides like a square and rectangle share. You may draw a shape that has 4 equal sides but different angles.

7. When you are explaining the attributes of your shape, it is important that you identify how the attributes are different from the ones shown in question 5 in relation to the attributes of a quadrilateral. For example, if you drew a trapezoid, you may indicate that the trapezoid is a quadrilateral because it has 4 straight sides and 4 angles. However, it is different because not all sides are parallel or it does not have 4 right angles.

8. A rhombus and a rectangle share any of the following attributes: 4 straight sides, four angles, and a closed shape. You can use any of these shared attributes to describe how these shapes are related.

Partitioning Shapes to Represent a Fraction (G.A.2), pages 148–149

1. **D** This shape shows the area of each part as $\frac{1}{8}$ of the area of the whole shape. Choice A is not evenly portioned; therefore, the area of the fractional parts are not equal. Although choice C is broken into eighths, the shaded portion of the shape is not representing the area as $\frac{1}{8}$, but rather $\frac{2}{8}$ which is the same as $\frac{1}{4}$. In choice B, there are four equal parts out of 8, but the other part represents $\frac{1}{2}$. It is important that when showing equal area of the whole, each part is represented with equal areas.

2. **D** The shape is divided into 4 parts of equal area. Therefore, there are 4 equal parts to the whole. This is represented as $\frac{1}{4}$.

3. The shape should be divided into 8 equal parts. A rectangle can be divided into fourths and then split in half, it can have 8 bars horizontally or vertically of equal area parts. The shape can also be divided into 4 equal triangles, and divided again to create eighths. When partitioning a shape it is important that each part is made with an equal area.

4. **A** Each fractional part of the rectangle is partitioned into 8 equal area parts. Therefore, the fraction used to represent the equal area parts is $\frac{1}{8}$.

5. **C** $\frac{2}{6}$ of the shape is not shaded in. The shape represents that $\frac{2}{6}$ could also be

seen as $\frac{1}{3}$. However, this is not an option for you to choose. If you choose A or B, you are looking at the shaded region. Mark each unit that is shaded and nonshaded to help you visually determine the fractional part that is not shaded.

6. **False.** The shape does not show equal area parts. Although the shape is divided or partitioned into 3 parts, each part is not representing equal area. When shapes are divided to represent a fraction, they must be partitioned into equal area parts. This means that each part must have the same area of each unit within the whole shape.

7. **A** The shape is partitioned into 8 equal area parts. Four of the equal area parts are shaded. Therefore, there are 4 of 8 equal area parts shaded. When looking at the shape, you must be able to determine how the shape is partitioned into equal area parts. Once you are able to determine the number of equal parts, think about how many parts are not shaded (4) to determine that 4 more equal area parts are needed to make the whole.

MATH PRACTICE TEST, pages 152–164

1. The circle should have been equal partitioned into 8 equal parts. You could have drawn fourths and then split each part in half to create eighths. After partitioning the circle, you should have shaded in 6 of the 8 parts to represent 6 of the 8 parts of the whole are shaded. (NF.A.1)

2. **D** When marking a number line, 3 equal parts of 3 can also be expressed as $\frac{3}{3}$. The fraction $\frac{3}{3}$ is the same as 1 whole. The fraction $\frac{3}{3}$ indicates that the whole is partitioned into thirds, in which there are 3 equal parts of the whole shaded or represented. Therefore, the entire whole is represented. (NF.A.2)

3. **C** The clock shows 1:53. When reading an analog clock, it is important that you are able to determine what the minute and hour hands are pointing to when reading the clock. The numbers on the clock are marked at every 5 minutes. The lines in between the 5 minutes are in 1 minute intervals. (MD.A.1)

4. **B** A kilogram is about the same weight as a baseball bat. A paperclip and dollar bill are about the same weight as a gram. The unit of a ton should be used to measure the mass of an elephant. (MD.A.2)

5. **B** In order to find the area of the shaded region, you would need to count how many squares there are across and how many there are up and down. There are 5 squares across and 6 up and down. This could be represented by 6×5 or $6 + 6 + 6 + 6 + 6$ or $5 + 5 + 5 + 5 + 5 + 5$. (MD.C.5)

6. Yes, the area of her wall is 42 square feet, and the area of the painting is 30 square feet. Therefore, the wall is larger than the painting. The area of the painting was determined by 10×3. (MD.C.7)

7. **A** The area of the shaded region is 5 square units. You can find this by adding up all of the squares in the shaded region. When doing this there are 3 across and 2 below. (MD.C.6)

8. **B** You should choose the answer that represents 4 groups of 5 as written in multiplication format. This can be represented by using repeated addition to add 4 groups of 5: $5 + 5 + 5 + 5$. Misconceptions could exist if you believe that you can use the repeated addition equation of adding 5 groups of 4; although this yields the same product, it does not accurately match the multiplication equation of 4×5. (OA.A.1)

9. **A** The whole shape is partitioned into 8 equal parts. Therefore, the area of each equal part is $\frac{1}{8}$ of the area of the whole unit or shape. (G.A.2)

10. You should draw a picture to accurately represent each equation. $48 \div 8 = 6$ should be represented by taking 48 items and dividing or sharing them into 8 equal groups with 6 in each group. $48 \div 6 = 8$ should be represented by taking 48 items and dividing or sharing them into 6 equal groups with 8

in each group. The order of the integers in these equations impacts the picture that is represented. (OA.A.2)

11. Samantha will earn $28 for babysitting. You should model your thinking with a picture first determining that if Samantha babysits from 6–10 P.M., she will babysit for 4 hours. You should then model that each of these hours or groups will earn her $7. Therefore, you are solving for the equation 4×7 and can solve this using repeated addition, skip counting, or using your fact fluency knowledge. (OA.A.3)

12. **C** You should determine the missing factor by determining if there are 7 groups, what equal amount should be in each group in order to make 21 in all. You could also use your understanding of the commutative property of multiplication to reverse the factors and determine the number of equal groups of 7 in 21 by using repeated addition or skip counting. (OA.A.4)

13. **$6 \times 7 = 42$** You should explain that the commutative property of multiplication means that the factors of a product can be written in any order and the product remains equal. Therefore, you reversed the factors in the product 7×6 to write the product 6×7. The equations would be represented visually in a different way: 7 groups of 6 or 6 groups of 7; however, both representations will have a total product of 42. (OA.B.5)

14. **C** You should be looking for an equation that matches the division equation using the same integers. Students should understand multiplication and division as inverse operations and that the product of a multiplication equation can become the dividend of a division equation. Knowing that these operations are related allows you to use the inverse operation to help you solve equations. (OA.B.6)

15. Yes, Matt will be able to fit all of the students into the video because they will use 45 seconds for their clips. There will be 15 seconds left over in the video. You should model your thinking by first determining how much time the student clips will take. You should show

an understanding that there are 9 students who each get 5 seconds; therefore, this can be solved using multiplication. You should find the product of $9 \times 5 = 45$. This determines the total seconds used for the video. Since 45 is less than 60, you know that there is enough time to fit all of the students into the 60-second video. The second part of the problem asks you to find out how much extra time is left on the video. This means you will be comparing 45 to 60 and using subtraction or missing addend addition to find the time left over. $60 - 45 = 15$ or $45 + \underline{\quad} = 60$. (OA.D.8)

16. You should have completed the chart as below:

Input	Output
10	20
5	**10**
7	14
6	12

Rule: $\times 2$, each input number is multiplied by 2 to find the output. (OA.D.9)

17. You can partition the rectangle into 4 equal parts in various ways. When partitioning the whole, it is important that each part of the whole is of equal area. In order to show $\frac{3}{4}$ you should have shaded in 3 of the 4 parts. The fraction $\frac{3}{4}$ is formed by shading in 3 of the 4 parts. (NF.A.1)

18. **B** When placing parts of a whole on a number line, 1 is the same as $\frac{4}{4}$. The dot indicates $\frac{3}{4}$ and $\frac{4}{4}$ is $\frac{1}{4}$ equal part away from $\frac{3}{4}$. Answer A, $\frac{1}{4}$, is 2 equal parts away from $\frac{3}{4}$ ($\frac{1}{4}, \frac{2}{4}, \frac{3}{4}$). Answers C and D are less than half of a whole. Therefore, since $\frac{3}{4}$ is greater than a half, this fraction is closer to the whole. (NF.A.2)

19. **A** The 2 number line models are representing that $\frac{1}{2}$ is the same as $\frac{2}{4}$. This indicates that they are equivalent. An equivalent fraction means that the fractions

are equal or the same. Although $\frac{2}{4}$ is made of larger numbers, the fractional part 2 equal parts of 4 is the same as the fractional part 1 equal part of 2. (NF.A.3)

20 and 21. You should place an = symbol in the box for question 20. These two fractions are equivalent. They both represent all parts of the whole. When justifying your answer, you should draw one rectangle into thirds and the other into sixths. You should have 6 equal parts of 6 shaded in to show the fraction $\frac{6}{6}$, and the same should be represented of the thirds. Therefore, the entire rectangle after it is partitioned should be shaded in. This will justify how you know that these two fractions are equal. (NF.A.3)

22. **A** Cooper was at practice for 1 hour and 14 minutes. You should have demonstrated this by using a number line. If you started the number line at 5:33 and hopped 1 hour, you would have landed on 6:33. You could then make a hop of 10 minutes, which would put you on 6:43. If you know that 4 and 3 make 7, then in order to have 43 minutes, you need 4 more minutes to get to 47. You could then combine, 1 hour and 10 minutes with the 4 minutes to get the answer of 1 hour and 14 minutes. (MD.A.1)

23. **D** You could measure the water in your tub by gallons. If you used cups or ounces, this would not be an efficient or accurate method to measure. These units are used to measure smaller amounts. A pound is not used to measure a liquid, but rather a solid figure. (MD.A.2)

24. **A** The answer is 24 square units because the question states that if a figure is covered with no space, gaps, or overlaps, then the area is the number of units it takes to cover that space. (MD.C.5)

25. **C** The number of single units that are covering up a given space. When calculating the area, you are finding how many single units are needed to cover a given space with no gaps, no space, and no overlaps. (MD.C.6)

26. You should draw a picture that models 8 groups of 2. Possible pictures could include drawing 8 faces with 2 eyes each, 8 plates with 2 cookies each, or 8 pairs of shoes with 2 shoes in each pair. (OA.A.1)

27. **A** This can be found by multiplying 9×2 which is 18 and 5×3, which is 15. Once you have the area of the two rectangles in the shape, you then add them together. $18 + 15$ is 33; therefore, the total area of the cafeteria is 33 square units. (MD.C.7)

28. **B** You should choose the answer that represents a division equation, which eliminates choices A and D. You are then looking at the total number of flowers and how they are grouped into the bouquets. There are 28 total flowers and they are in 7 bouquets, so the equation $28 \div 7$ accurately matches this picture. (OA.A.2)

29. Norah will need 30 corn plants for her garden. You should draw a picture that shows an array with 6 rows and 5 plants in each row. When you have completed the array, you should then see this as a representation of multiplication and find the product. You can find the product of these rows using repeated addition or by grouping the rows into more easy-to-add sums; such as making groups of 10 from 2 rows of 5. You should use the multiplication equation $6 \times 5 = 30$ to model the 6 rows with 5 plants in each row. (OA.A.3)

30. You should determine the missing divisor is 9 by using your knowledge of multiplication and division as inverse operations. When you are given the dividend and the quotient, you can use these to set up a missing factor multiplication equation: $5 \times \underline{\quad} = 45$ and use your multiplication strategies to determine how many items would be in each of 5 equal groups to total 45. (OA.A.4)

31. The associative property of multiplication means that you can group factors in an equation with more than 2 factors in any way in order to more easily multiply and solve the equation. You could solve this equation by first solving $7 \times 2 = 14$ (you could choose to solve a $\times 2$ equation first because you more easily know your doubles and then multiply 14×5). You could also start with multiplying $7 \times 5 = 35$ (you could choose to solve the

× 5 equation first and then you could more easily double the product of 35 × 2). Finally, you could also group 5 × 2 = 10 to solve first and then more easily multiply the product 10 × 7 as you can easily multiply by 10. (OA.B.5)

32. The missing number is 6 to make both equations true. You should explain how the multiplication and division equations are related. You should demonstrate how a multiplication equation's factors could be used to find the quotient of a division equation. Multiplication and division are inverse operations and therefore the integers in the equations are related. (OA.B.6)

33. Lucy will have $9 left over to spend on rides. You should model your thinking with a picture to show all of the items that Lucy purchased and the cost of each item. You can show the total cost by using addition: 17 + 6 + 9 + 9 = 41. Therefore, Lucy spent $41 at the festival. The question then asks how much money Lucy will have left over. You should then subtract the $41 that she spent from the $50 she brought: 50 − 41 = $9 left over. (OA.D.8)

34. You should explain that the first equation has 6 groups of 2 and the second equation has 6 groups of 4. The second factor in this division equation has doubled and this can also be modeled using the distributive property of multiplication to break 6 × 4 into 6 × 2 and 6 × 2. Therefore, you can use the product of 6 × 2 to double and find the product of 6 × 4.

    6 × 2 = 12
    6 × 4 = 12 + 12 = 24
    (OA.D.9)

35. **A** The number of equal parts in a fraction describe how many equal parts are used to make the whole. The number of equal parts used is determined by how the whole is partitioned. (NF.A.1)

36. **C** The number line is partitioned into eight equal parts. Although $\frac{1}{2}$ is shown on the number line, the line is portioned into more equal parts than 2. (NF.A.2)

37. **True.** The fraction $\frac{4}{1}$ is representing the whole number 4 as a fraction. Whole

numbers can be represented as a fraction. Additionally, fractions such as $\frac{4}{4}$ can be represented as a whole number 1. (NF.A.3)

38. **C** Austin arrives each day at 7:17 A.M. Using the number line model, if you start on the right side and label it 7:50, then take 3 hops of 10 minutes (representing 30 minutes) you will land on 7:20. Next, subtract 3 from 20, and you will land on 17. Therefore, Austin arrives each day at 7:17 A.M. When writing time, it is important to include A.M. or P.M. Since this problem discussed what happens in the morning, you need to use A.M. (MD.A.1)

39. **B** The problem asked what are the total grams of fat for the pizza, not just the meat. The student needed to find the grams of fat that are from the meat and combine this with the grams of fat from the cheese. There are 48 grams of fat from the meat (6 × 8 = 48). Then you needed to add 6 grams of fat from the cheese to 48 grams of fat from the meat to get a total of 54 grams of fat. (MD.A.2)

40. **B** The answer is found by multiplying 9 × 4 or using repeated addition. (MD.C.5)

41. **D** You should use the picture and determine that there are 6 groups represented by the 6 gumball machines. You will then need to count and find how many gumballs are in each group or machine. You should find that each machine has 9 gumballs; therefore, this picture represents the equation 6 × 9 or 6 groups of 9. (OA.A.1)

42. There should be 28 unit squares in the rectangle. The unit squares should not be overlapped. They should have no spaces or gaps between. This should be drawn as 7 columns and 4 rows. To prove your answer, you should express that you counted each individual unit or that you multiplied 7 × 4, or used repeated addition to determine the area. (MD.C.6)

43. **C** Clarence could also use multiplication to represent repeated addition. It is important that you are able to make the connection between multiplication and addition, along with how this can be represented when finding the area of a space. (MD.C.7)

44. Story problem contexts may vary depending on your response. In the story problem you should describe how a total of 24 items are shared among 4 groups. The problem asks for you specifically to use sharing so if you were to write a story problem about taking the 24 items and putting them in groups of 4 this would inaccurately match the problem. A sample story problem could be: Matt brings 24 trading cards to school. He shares the cards with 4 friends. How many cards will they each get? (OA.A.2)

45. **They can make 9 equal teams of players.** You should draw a picture modeling 54 players grouped into equal groups of 6 in order to determine how many equal groups of 6 can be created from the 54 players. You should model your thinking with the division equation $54 \div 6 = 9$ to show that you are taking 54 players and grouping them into equal groups of 6, which will make 9 equal groups. Then you should explain how you solved the problem using words to tell your strategy for determining the equal groups: repeated subtraction, drawing a model and grouping the 54 players into equal groups of 6, or using multiplication as the inverse operation to find the number of groups of 6 in 54. (OA.A.3)

46. You should complete the multiplication equations:

    $4 \times 8 = 32, 8 \times 4 = 32$

    You should complete the division equations:
    $32 \div 4 = 8, 32 \div 8 = 4$

    You should use your knowledge of multiplication and division as inverse (opposite) operations. You should also have an understanding that when writing a multiplication equation, the factors would be multiplied to reach the product and the product will be the greater number. The same understanding can be applied to writing division equations in which you start with the whole (greater number) as the divisor. (OA.A.4)

47. **Grace can use the equation 8×1 to help her solve 8×6.** She can use the distributive property of multiplication in which you can break apart one of the factors and multiply each integer by the remaining factor in order to find the total product. Grace can break the factor 6 into $5 + 1$ and since she knows 8×5 she can also solve 8×1 and then add these two products.

    $8 \times 5 = 40$ and $8 \times 1 = 8$, so $40 + 8 = 48 = 8 \times 6$

    (OA.B.5)

48. You should write the equation $27 \div 3 = 9$ or $27 \div 9 = 3$ as the related division equation for $9 \times 3 = 27$. You should write the equation $6 \times 3 = 18$ or $3 \times 6 = 18$ as the related multiplication equation for $18 \div 3 = 6$. Division and multiplication equations are related as inverse operations and you should create equations that use the same integers. The quotient and divisor become the factors in the multiplication equation to make the dividend or product. The factors become the quotient and the divisor in the division equation and the product becomes the dividend. (OA.B.6)

49. He can share his cookies with 21 friends. You should model your thinking with a picture to first show the total amount of cookies bought. You should add $24 + 18 = 42$ total cookies to share. You can model your strategy for addition using place value; for example: $20 + 10 = 30$, $4 + 8 = 12$, so $30 + 12 = 42$. You should then take the 42 total cookies and group them into sets of 2 because each friend gets 2 cookies. When you group the cookies, you should be able to determine the total number of equal groups that can be made using a picture or division equation: $42 \div 2 = 21$. (OA.D.8)

50. You should explain that the equation 9×10 could be used to help solve 9×9. You have one less in each of the 9 groups when you compare the equations 9×10 and 9×9; therefore, you can find the product of 9×10 and then subtract 9 from this product to find 9×9. You know the equation 9×10 and therefore you can quickly solve 9×9 using this strategy.

    $9 \times 10 = 90$, so $9 \times 9 = 90 - 9 = 81$

    (OA.D.9)

APPENDIX A
ENGLISH LANGUAGE ARTS STANDARDS

Reading: Literature
CCSS.ELA-Literacy.RL.3.1 Ask and answer questions to demonstrate understanding of a text, referring explicitly to the text as the basis for the answers.
CCSS.ELA-Literacy.RL.3.2 Recount stories, including fables, folktales, and myths from diverse cultures; determine the central message, lesson, or moral and explain how it is conveyed through key details in the text.
CCSS.ELA-Literacy.RL.3.3 Describe characters in a story (e.g., their traits, motivations, or feelings) and explain how their actions contribute to the sequence of events.
CCSS.ELA-Literacy.RL.3.4 Determine the meaning of words and phrases as they are used in a text, distinguishing literal from nonliteral language.
CCSS.ELA-Literacy.RL.3.5 Refer to parts of stories, dramas, and poems when writing or speaking about a text, using terms such as chapter, scene, and stanza; describe how each successive part builds on earlier sections.
CCSS.ELA-Literacy.RL.3.6 Distinguish their own point of view from that of the narrator or those of the characters.
CCSS.ELA-Literacy.RL.3.7 Explain how specific aspects of a text's illustrations contribute to what is conveyed by the words in a story (e.g., create mood, emphasize aspects of a character or setting).
CCSS.ELA-Literacy.RL.3.9 Compare and contrast the themes, settings, and plots of stories written by the same author about the same or similar characters (e.g., in books from a series).
CCSS.ELA-Literacy.RL.3.10 By the end of the year, read and comprehend literature, including stories, dramas, and poetry, at the high end of the grades 2–3 text complexity band independently and proficiently.
Reading: Informational Text
CCSS.ELA-Literacy.RI.3.1 Ask and answer questions to demonstrate understanding of a text, referring explicitly to the text as the basis for the answers.
CCSS.ELA-Literacy.RI.3.2 Determine the main idea of a text; recount the key details and explain how they support the main idea.
CCSS.ELA-Literacy.RI.3.3 Describe the relationship between a series of historical events, scientific ideas or concepts, or steps in technical procedures in a text, using language that pertains to time, sequence, and cause/effect.
CCSS.ELA-Literacy.RI.3.4 Determine the meaning of general academic and domain-specific words and phrases in a text relevant to a *grade 3 topic or subject area*.
CCSS.ELA-Literacy.RI.3.5 Use text features and search tools (e.g., key words, sidebars, hyperlinks) to locate information relevant to a given topic efficiently.
CCSS.ELA-Literacy.RI.3.6 Distinguish their own point of view from that of the author of a text.
CCSS.ELA-Literacy.RI.3.7 Use information gained from illustrations (e.g., maps, photographs) and the words in a text to demonstrate understanding of the text (e.g., where, when, why, and how key events occur).
CCSS.ELA-Literacy.RI.3.8 Describe the logical connection between particular sentences and paragraphs in a text (e.g., comparison, cause/effect, first/second/third in a sequence).

CCSS.ELA-Literacy.RI.3.9 Compare and contrast the most important points and key details presented in two texts on the same topic.

CCSS.ELA-Literacy.RI.3.10 By the end of the year, read and comprehend informational texts, including history/social studies, science, and technical texts, at the high end of the grades 2–3 text complexity band independently and proficiently.

Reading: Foundational Skills

CCSS.ELA-Literacy.RF.3.3 Know and apply grade-level phonics and word analysis skills in decoding words.

CCSS.ELA-LITERACY.RF.3.3.A

Identify and know the meaning of the most common prefixes and derivational suffixes.

CCSS.ELA-LITERACY.RF.3.3.B

Decode words with common Latin suffixes.

CCSS.ELA-LITERACY.RF.3.3.C

Decode multisyllable words.

CCSS.ELA-LITERACY.RF.3.3.D

Read grade-appropriate irregularly spelled words.

CCSS.ELA-Literacy.RF.3.4 Read with sufficient accuracy and fluency to support comprehension.

CCSS.ELA-LITERACY.RF.3.4.A

Read grade-level text with purpose and understanding.

CCSS.ELA-LITERACY.RF.3.4.B

Read grade-level prose and poetry orally with accuracy, appropriate rate, and expression on successive readings.

CCSS.ELA-LITERACY.RF.3.4.C

Use context to confirm or self-correct word recognition and understanding, rereading as necessary.

Writing

CCSS.ELA-Literacy.W.3.1 Write opinion pieces on topics or texts, supporting a point of view with reasons.

CCSS.ELA-LITERACY.W.3.1.A

Introduce the topic or text they are writing about, state an opinion, and create an organizational structure that lists reasons.

CCSS.ELA-LITERACY.W.3.1.B

Provide reasons that support the opinion.

CCSS.ELA-LITERACY.W.3.1.C

Use linking words and phrases (e.g., *because*, *therefore*, *since*, *for example*) to connect opinion and reasons.

CCSS.ELA-LITERACY.W.3.1.D

Provide a concluding statement or section.

CCSS.ELA-Literacy.W.3.2 Write informative/explanatory texts to examine a topic and convey ideas and information clearly.

CCSS.ELA-LITERACY.W.3.2.A

Introduce a topic and group related information together; include illustrations when useful to aiding comprehension.

CCSS.ELA-LITERACY.W.3.2.B

Develop the topic with facts, definitions, and details.

CCSS.ELA-LITERACY.W.3.2.C

Use linking words and phrases (e.g., *also*, *another*, *and*, *more*, *but*) to connect ideas within categories of information.

CCSS.ELA-LITERACY.W.3.2.D

Provide a concluding statement or section.

CCSS.ELA-Literacy.W.3.3 Write narratives to develop real or imagined experiences or events using effective technique, descriptive details, and clear event sequences.

> CCSS.ELA-LITERACY.W.3.3.A
>
> Establish a situation and introduce a narrator and/or characters; organize an event sequence that unfolds naturally.
>
> CCSS.ELA-LITERACY.W.3.3.B
>
> Use dialogue and descriptions of actions, thoughts, and feelings to develop experiences and events or show the response of characters to situations.
>
> CCSS.ELA-LITERACY.W.3.3.C
>
> Use temporal words and phrases to signal event order.
>
> CCSS.ELA-LITERACY.W.3.3.D
>
> Provide a sense of closure.

CCSS.ELA-Literacy.W.3.4 With guidance and support from adults, produce writing in which the development and organization are appropriate to task and purpose. (Grade-specific expectations for writing types are defined in standards 1–3 above.)

CCSS.ELA-Literacy.W.3.5 With guidance and support from peers and adults, develop and strengthen writing as needed by planning, revising, and editing. (Editing for conventions should demonstrate command of Language standards 1-3 up to and including grade 3 here.)

CCSS.ELA-Literacy.W.3.6 With guidance and support from adults, use technology to produce and publish writing (using keyboarding skills) as well as to interact and collaborate with others.

CCSS.ELA-Literacy.W.3.7 Conduct short research projects that build knowledge about a topic.

CCSS.ELA-Literacy.W.3.8 Recall information from experiences or gather information from print and digital sources; take brief notes on sources and sort evidence into provided categories.

CCSS.ELA-Literacy.W.3.10 Write routinely over extended time frames (time for research, reflection, and revision) and shorter time frames (a single sitting or a day or two) for a range of discipline-specific tasks, purposes, and audiences.

Speaking and Listening

CCSS.ELA-Literacy.SL.3.1 Engage effectively in a range of collaborative discussions (one-on-one, in groups, and teacher-led) with diverse partners on *grade 3 topics and texts*, building on others' ideas and expressing their own clearly.

> CCSS.ELA-LITERACY.SL.3.1.A
>
> Come to discussions prepared, having read or studied required material; explicitly draw on that preparation and other information known about the topic to explore ideas under discussion.
>
> CCSS.ELA-LITERACY.SL.3.1.B
>
> Follow agreed-upon rules for discussions (e.g., gaining the floor in respectful ways, listening to others with care, speaking one at a time about the topics and texts under discussion).
>
> CCSS.ELA-LITERACY.SL.3.1.C
>
> Ask questions to check understanding of information presented, stay on topic, and link their comments to the remarks of others.
>
> CCSS.ELA-LITERACY.SL.3.1.D
>
> Explain their own ideas and understanding in light of the discussion.

CCSS.ELA-Literacy.SL.3.2 Determine the main ideas and supporting details of a text read aloud or information presented in diverse media and formats, including visually, quantitatively, and orally.

CCSS.ELA-Literacy.SL.3.3 Ask and answer questions about information from a speaker, offering appropriate elaboration and detail.

CCSS.ELA-Literacy.SL.3.4 Report on a topic or text, tell a story, or recount an experience with appropriate facts and relevant, descriptive details, speaking clearly at an understandable pace.

CCSS.ELA-Literacy.SL.3.5 Create engaging audio recordings of stories or poems that demonstrate fluid reading at an understandable pace; add visual displays when appropriate to emphasize or enhance certain facts or details.

CCSS.ELA-Literacy.SL.3.6 Speak in complete sentences when appropriate to task and situation in order to provide requested detail or clarification. (See grade 3 Language standards 1 and 3 here for specific expectations.)

Language

CCSS.ELA-Literacy.L.3.1 Demonstrate command of the conventions of standard English grammar and usage when writing or speaking.

CCSS.ELA-LITERACY.L.3.1.A

Explain the function of nouns, pronouns, verbs, adjectives, and adverbs in general and their functions in particular sentences.

CCSS.ELA-LITERACY.L.3.1.B

Form and use regular and irregular plural nouns.

CCSS.ELA-LITERACY.L.3.1.C

Use abstract nouns (e.g., *childhood*).

CCSS.ELA-LITERACY.L.3.1.D

Form and use regular and irregular verbs.

CCSS.ELA-LITERACY.L.3.1.E

Form and use the simple (e.g., *I walked; I walk; I will walk*) verb tenses.

CCSS.ELA-LITERACY.L.3.1.F

Ensure subject-verb and pronoun-antecedent agreement.*

CCSS.ELA-LITERACY.L.3.1.G

Form and use comparative and superlative adjectives and adverbs, and choose between them depending on what is to be modified.

CCSS.ELA-LITERACY.L.3.1.H

Use coordinating and subordinating conjunctions.

CCSS.ELA-LITERACY.L.3.1.I

Produce simple, compound, and complex sentences.

CCSS.ELA-Literacy.L.3.2 Demonstrate command of the conventions of standard English capitalization, punctuation, and spelling when writing.

CCSS.ELA-LITERACY.L.3.2.A

Capitalize appropriate words in titles.

CCSS.ELA-LITERACY.L.3.2.B

Use commas in addresses.

CCSS.ELA-LITERACY.L.3.2.C

Use commas and quotation marks in dialogue.

CCSS.ELA-LITERACY.L.3.2.D

Form and use possessives.

CCSS.ELA-LITERACY.L.3.2.E

Use conventional spelling for high-frequency and other studied words and for adding suffixes to base words (e.g., *sitting, smiled, cries, happiness*).

CCSS.ELA-LITERACY.L.3.2.F

Use spelling patterns and generalizations (e.g., *word families, position-based spellings, syllable patterns, ending rules, meaningful word parts*) in writing words.

CCSS.ELA-LITERACY.L.3.2.G

Consult reference materials, including beginning dictionaries, as needed to check and correct spellings.

CCSS.ELA-Literacy.L.3.3 Use knowledge of language and its conventions when writing, speaking, reading, or listening.

CCSS.ELA-LITERACY.L.3.3.A

Choose words and phrases for effect.*

CCSS.ELA-LITERACY.L.3.3.B

Recognize and observe differences between the conventions of spoken and written standard English.

CCSS.ELA-Literacy.L.3.4 Determine or clarify the meaning of unknown and multiple-meaning words and phrases based on grade 3 reading and content, choosing flexibly from a range of strategies.

CCSS.ELA-LITERACY.L.3.4.A

Use sentence-level context as a clue to the meaning of a word or phrase.

CCSS.ELA-LITERACY.L.3.4.B

Determine the meaning of the new word formed when a known affix is added to a known word (e.g., *agreeable/disagreeable, comfortable/uncomfortable, care/careless, heat/preheat*).

CCSS.ELA-LITERACY.L.3.4.C

Use a known root word as a clue to the meaning of an unknown word with the same root (e.g., *company, companion*).

CCSS.ELA-LITERACY.L.3.4.D

Use glossaries or beginning dictionaries, both print and digital, to determine or clarify the precise meaning of key words and phrases.

CCSS.ELA-Literacy.L.3.5 Demonstrate understanding of figurative language, word relationships, and nuances in word meanings.

CCSS.ELA-LITERACY.L.3.5.A

Distinguish the literal and nonliteral meanings of words and phrases in context (e.g., *take steps*).

CCSS.ELA-LITERACY.L.3.5.B

Identify real-life connections between words and their use (e.g., describe people who are *friendly* or *helpful*).

CCSS.ELA-LITERACY.L.3.5.C

Distinguish shades of meaning among related words that describe states of mind or degrees of certainty (e.g., *knew, believed, suspected, heard, wondered*).

CCSS.ELA-Literacy.L.3.6 Acquire and use accurately grade-appropriate conversational, general academic, and domain-specific words and phrases, including those that signal spatial and temporal relationships (e.g., *After dinner that night we went looking for them*).

APPENDIX B
MATH STANDARDS

Operations and Algebraic Thinking

CCSS.Math.Content.3.OA.A.1 Interpret products of whole numbers, e.g., interpret 5 × 7 as the total number of objects in 5 groups of 7 objects each. *For example, describe a context in which a total number of objects can be expressed as 5 × 7.*

CCSS.Math.Content.3.OA.A.2 Interpret whole-number quotients of whole numbers, e.g., interpret 56 ÷ 8 as the number of objects in each share when 56 objects are partitioned equally into 8 shares, or as a number of shares when 56 objects are partitioned into equal shares of 8 objects each. *For example, describe a context in which a number of shares or a number of groups can be expressed as 56 ÷ 8.*

CCSS.Math.Content.3.OA.A.3 Use multiplication and division within 100 to solve word problems in situations involving equal groups, arrays, and measurement quantities, e.g., by using drawings and equations with a symbol for the unknown number to represent the problem.

CCSS.Math.Content.3.OA.A.4 Determine the unknown whole number in a multiplication or division equation relating three whole numbers. *For example, determine the unknown number that makes the equation true in each of the equations 8 × ? = 48, 5 = _ ÷ 3, 6 × 6 = ?*

CCSS.Math.Content.3.OA.B.5 Apply properties of operations as strategies to multiply and divide. *Examples: If 6 × 4 = 24 is known, then 4 × 6 = 24 is also known. (Commutative property of multiplication.) 3 × 5 × 2 can be found by 3 × 5 = 15, then 15 × 2 = 30, or by 5 × 2 = 10, then 3 × 10 = 30. (Associative property of multiplication.) Knowing that 8 × 5 = 40 and 8 × 2 = 16, one can find 8 × 7 as 8 × (5 + 2) = (8 × 5) + (8 × 2) = 40 + 16 = 56. (Distributive property.)*

CCSS.Math.Content.3.OA.B.6 Understand division as an unknown-factor problem. *For example, find 32 ÷ 8 by finding the number that makes 32 when multiplied by 8.*

CCSS.Math.Content.3.OA.C.7 Fluently multiply and divide within 100, using strategies such as the relationship between multiplication and division (e.g., knowing that 8 × 5 = 40, one knows 40 ÷ 5 = 8) or properties of operations. By the end of Grade 3, know from memory all products of two one-digit numbers.

CCSS.Math.Content.3.OA.D.8 Solve two-step word problems using the four operations. Represent these problems using equations with a letter standing for the unknown quantity. Assess the reasonableness of answers using mental computation and estimation strategies including rounding.

CCSS.Math.Content.3.OA.D.9 Identify arithmetic patterns (including patterns in the addition table or multiplication table), and explain them using properties of operations. *For example, observe that 4 times a number is always even, and explain why 4 times a number can be decomposed into two equal addends.*

Number and Operations in Base Ten

CCSS.Math.Content.3.NBT.A.1 Use place value understanding to round whole numbers to the nearest 10 or 100.

CCSS.Math.Content.3.NBT.A.2 Fluently add and subtract within 1000 using strategies and algorithms based on place value, properties of operations, and/or the relationship between addition and subtraction.

CCSS.Math.Content.3.NBT.A.3 Multiply one-digit whole numbers by multiples of 10 in the range 10–90 (e.g., 9 × 80, 5 × 60) using strategies based on place value and properties of operations.

Number and Operations—Fractions

CCSS.Math.Content.3.NF.A.1 Understand a fraction 1/*b* as the quantity formed by 1 part when a whole is partitioned into *b* equal parts; understand a fraction *a*/*b* as the quantity formed by *a* parts of size 1/*b*.

CCSS.Math.Content.3.NF.A.2 Understand a fraction as a number on the number line; represent fractions on a number line diagram.

CCSS.MATH.CONTENT.3.NF.A.2.A

Represent a fraction 1/*b* on a number line diagram by defining the interval from 0 to 1 as the whole and partitioning it into *b* equal parts. Recognize that each part has size 1/*b* and that the endpoint of the part based at 0 locates the number 1/*b* on the number line.

CCSS.MATH.CONTENT.3.NF.A.2.B

Represent a fraction *a*/*b* on a number line diagram by marking off *a* lengths 1/*b* from 0. Recognize that the resulting interval has size *a*/*b* and that its endpoint locates the number *a*/*b* on the number line.

CCSS.Math.Content.3.NF.A.3 Explain equivalence of fractions in special cases, and compare fractions by reasoning about their size.

CCSS.MATH.CONTENT.3.NF.A.3.A

Understand two fractions as equivalent (equal) if they are the same size, or the same point on a number line.

CCSS.MATH.CONTENT.3.NF.A.3.B

Recognize and generate simple equivalent fractions, e.g., 1/2 = 2/4, 4/6 = 2/3. Explain why the fractions are equivalent, e.g., by using a visual fraction model.

CCSS.MATH.CONTENT.3.NF.A.3.C

Express whole numbers as fractions, and recognize fractions that are equivalent to whole numbers. *Examples: Express 3 in the form 3 = 3/1; recognize that 6/1 = 6; locate 4/4 and 1 at the same point of a number line diagram.*

CCSS.MATH.CONTENT.3.NF.A.3.D

Compare two fractions with the same numerator or the same denominator by reasoning about their size. Recognize that comparisons are valid only when the two fractions refer to the same whole. Record the results of comparisons with the symbols >, =, or <, and justify the conclusions, e.g., by using a visual fraction model.

Measurement and Data

CCSS.Math.Content.3.MD.A.1 Tell and write time to the nearest minute and measure time intervals in minutes. Solve word problems involving addition and subtraction of time intervals in minutes, e.g., by representing the problem on a number line diagram.

CCSS.Math.Content.3.MD.A.2 Measure and estimate liquid volumes and masses of objects using standard units of grams (g), kilograms (kg), and liters (l). Add, subtract, multiply, or divide to solve one-step word problems involving masses or volumes that are given in the same units, e.g., by using drawings (such as a beaker with a measurement scale) to represent the problem.

CCSS.Math.Content.3.MD.B.3 Draw a scaled picture graph and a scaled bar graph to represent a data set with several categories. Solve one- and two-step "how many more" and "how many less" problems using information presented in scaled bar graphs. *For example, draw a bar graph in which each square in the bar graph might represent 5 pets.*

CCSS.Math.Content.3.MD.B.4 Generate measurement data by measuring lengths using rulers marked with halves and fourths of an inch. Show the data by making a line plot, where the horizontal scale is marked off in appropriate units—whole numbers, halves, or quarters.

CCSS.Math.Content.3.MD.C.5 Recognize area as an attribute of plane figures and understand concepts of area measurement.

> CCSS.MATH.CONTENT.3.MD.C.5.A
>
> A square with side length 1 unit, called "a unit square," is said to have "one square unit" of area, and can be used to measure area.
>
> CCSS.MATH.CONTENT.3.MD.C.5.B
>
> A plane figure which can be covered without gaps or overlaps by n unit squares is said to have an area of n square units.

CCSS.Math.Content.3.MD.C.6 Measure areas by counting unit squares (square cm, square m, square in, square ft, and improvised units).

CCSS.Math.Content.3.MD.C.7 Relate area to the operations of multiplication and addition.

> CCSS.MATH.CONTENT.3.MD.C.7.A
>
> Find the area of a rectangle with whole-number side lengths by tiling it, and show that the area is the same as would be found by multiplying the side lengths.
>
> CCSS.MATH.CONTENT.3.MD.C.7.B
>
> Multiply side lengths to find areas of rectangles with whole-number side lengths in the context of solving real world and mathematical problems, and represent whole-number products as rectangular areas in mathematical reasoning.
>
> CCSS.MATH.CONTENT.3.MD.C.7.C
>
> Use tiling to show in a concrete case that the area of a rectangle with whole-number side lengths a and $b + c$ is the sum of $a \times b$ and $a \times c$. Use area models to represent the distributive property in mathematical reasoning.
>
> CCSS.MATH.CONTENT.3.MD.C.7.D
>
> Recognize area as additive. Find areas of rectilinear figures by decomposing them into nonoverlapping rectangles and adding the areas of the nonoverlapping parts, applying this technique to solve real world problems.

CCSS.Math.Content.3.MD.D.8 Solve real world and mathematical problems involving perimeters of polygons, including finding the perimeter given the side lengths, finding an unknown side length, and exhibiting rectangles with the same perimeter and different areas or with the same area and different perimeters.

Geometry

CCSS.Math.Content.3.G.A.1 Understand that shapes in different categories (e.g., rhombuses, rectangles, and others) may share attributes (e.g., having four sides), and that the shared attributes can define a larger category (e.g., quadrilaterals). Recognize rhombuses, rectangles, and squares as examples of quadrilaterals, and draw examples of quadrilaterals that do not belong to any of these subcategories.

CCSS.Math.Content.3.G.A.2 Partition shapes into parts with equal areas. Express the area of each part as a unit fraction of the whole. *For example, partition a shape into 4 parts with equal area, and describe the area of each part as 1/4 of the area of the shape.*

NOTES

NOTES

NOTES

NOTES

NOTES

NOTES

NOTES

NOTES